Internet Resources:
A Subject Guide

Updated and revised from articles originally appearing in
College & Research Libraries News

A publication of the
Association of College & Research Libraries
a division of the American Library Association

Compiled by
Hugh A. Thompson

ASSOCIATION OF

COLLEGE
& RESEARCH
LIBRARIES
A DIVISION OF THE
AMERICAN LIBRARY ASSOCIATION

Published by the Association of College and
Research Libraries
A Division of the American Library Association
50 East Huron Street
Chicago, IL 60611
1-800-545-2433

ISBN 0-8389-7785-5

Table of Contents

Preface

Since its advent, the Internet has grown from a simple emergency method of communications to an enormous web comprised of both users and computer networks. The Internet has facilitated an information revolution that was already well underway before it began its exponential growth. But some of the advantages of the Internet, such as the ready availability of copious amounts of information, have also led to a certain degree of frustration and chaos, the search capabilities of the net notwithstanding. The Internet has come to resemble a library in which each of the individual volumes are being revised continually, and many new volumes are being added as well. All of this is occurring on an enormous scale, and the pace of change is so great, the catalog cannot possibly be kept up-to-date.

In April, 1993, *College & Research Libraries News*, the official news magazine of the Association of College and Research Libraries, began running a series of articles on Internet resources. Each article addresses a single subject area and lists extensive sources for access, such as gophers, listservs, online bibliographies, discussion groups, newsletters, world wide web sites and more. This book is a collection of sixteen of those articles on a wide range of topics. Authors were given an opportunity to update their articles at the time of publication, so that much of the information in this compilation is new. No print publication about the Internet can hope to remain current given the speed with which changes occur, but many resources listed here remain valid. They may also serve as a starting point that will lead to any additional information that has become available since publication.

Internet resources for architecture studies

Jeanne Brown

Introduction

As I write this in December of 1994, almost two years after submitting the short piece "Internet resources for architecture studies" which appeared in the April 1993 *College & Research Libraries News*, I am struck by the dramatic increase in the number and nature of the resources in architecture currently accessible on the Internet. The resources two years ago were primarily library databases and discussion groups. Only one gopher was listed. No web sites were identified. Today gopher and web sites are the heart of any list of Internet resources. And "today" has just recently arrived. Even the period of the last six months has seen substantial changes as web sites proliferate. There is, in fact, little resemblance between this list and the one published in April 1993.

There are so many resources that this list must be a highly selective one. I have chosen sites representative of the various categories of architecture resources: general web sites; web sites focused on architectural computing; image sites; library contributions including opacs, gophers, indexes and special databases, and web sites; electronic journals and newsletters; listservs and newsgroups; university architecture program sites; and information on accessibility and universal design. Within those categories, the ones which offer original contributions or approaches, or are typical of the category, were selected.

Jeanne Brown is architecture studies librarian at the University of Nevada, Las Vegas; e-mail: jeanneb@nevada.edu

A more extensive list compiled by this author (but still selected, the Internet defying anyone who would call their efforts "complete") is posted on the Internet at the University of Michigan Clearinghouse for Subject-Oriented Internet Resource Guides (URL: gopher://una.hh.lib.umich.edu/70/ 00 inetdirsstacks/archi:brown; Address: gopher una.hh.lib.umich.edu inetdirsstacks/Architecture). Marco Vlemmix prepares a hypertext version of the list posted at the University of Michigan and makes it available at LAVA, The Lab for Architects (URL: http://www.tue.nl/lava/other/brown inttoc.html). These lists are updated periodically.

WORLD WIDE WEB SITES

• The Center for Landscape Research University of Toronto (URL: http:/ www.clr.toronto.edu:1080) is an excellent starting point for surfing or browsing the web, and the most comprehensive set of links to architecture and landscape architecture sites. CLRnet provides the web's architecture and landscape architecture virtual library subject index (the architecture list is subdivided by topics such as jobs, conferences, competitions, schools, government agencies, research, firms, history, projects, information sources, software, news groups, mail lists, landscape architecture, and engineering). The Center for Landscape Research site also provides an archive of theses in landscape architecture.

• LAVA, The Lab for Architects, Technische Universiteit Eindhoven, Faculty of Architecture and Planning (URL: http://www.tue.nl/lava) "features de sign projects, texts, discussions etc.," including book reviews. While parts are still obviously under construction (such as the mail from selected lists June-August 1994), this is a site which is constantly changing and trying new approaches. Its most recent experiment is a virtual studio (temporary URL: http://w3.urc.tue.nl/lava/studio.html). It also offers access to its gopher as well as other pointers to net information. Information about departments and institutes at the university can be found at URL: http:/ www.tue.nl/ bwk. The section on the Calibre Institute is of interest, with several images and research documents related to their work on multimedia and virtual reality.

• The Imaging Systems Laboratory, Department of Landscape Architecture, University of Illinois, Urbana-Champaign (URL:http:/ imlab9.landarch.uiuc. edu) has "concentrated on environmental perception research related to the visualization of environmental impacts, with emphases on methodological studies and on preference and choice modeling." This substantive site includes full-text of publications for most projects, lists of publications and grants received, and bibliographies in the lab's areas of research.

• The RMIT (Royal Melbourne Institute of Technology) National Key Centre for Design (URL: http://daedalus.edc.rmit.edu.au) "exists to focus the work of Australian designers, researchers, industry and government on the changing relationship between design, production and consumption." This site provides Centre research papers and projects such as EcoReDesign ("a program to improve the environmental performance of manufactured prod ucts") and Eco Built Environment ("an inquiry into the philosophy of environmental sustainability both for the design and the designers of the built environment") as well as links to other environmental design research centers, and to Internet sites relating to the built environment.

• Columbia University has several sites of interest: the Graduate School of Architecture (URL: http://www.cc.columbia.edu/~archpub), the Digital De sign Lab (URL: http:// www.arch.columbia.edu), and the AcIS Imaging and Hypertext Projects (URL: http://gutentag.cc.columbia.edu/imaging/html imaging.html). In addition, syllabi for some of its architecture courses are posted, including one, the Seminar on Technology Transfer in Architecture, which provides a hypertext document leading to pertinent sites on the net! (URL: http://www.cc.columbia.edu/courses/courses.html).

Web Sites: Architectural Computing
There are several sites whose primarily orientation is toward computing: the Ray Tracing Home Page (URL: http://www.cm.cf.ac.uk/Ray.Tracing) with Ray Tracing images, general information (including an annotated bibliography and a FAQ on ray tracing), and information on rendering packages; the University of New South Wales Faculty of the Built Environment (URL: http: /149.171.160.160/) which has a Rayshade Objects Library (use mosaic), in formation on the faculty, tutorials (including some on autocad and Rayshade), and undergraduate research papers; and the Radiance Home Page (URL: http://radsite.lbl.gov/radiance/HOME.html) which contains a description of the radiance ray-tracing software, sources on the Internet from which to obtain it, tips for using it, an archive of a radiance discussion group, and other www sites featuring radiance. Another computing-oriented site is SEED, which stands for Software Environment to support the Early phases in building Design. "The modules envisioned for the first SEED prototype support the following phases: architectural programming, schematic layout design, and schematic configuration design." (URL: http:/ logan.edrc.cmu.edu: 8001/ OverView.html).

Library Contributions
The most frequently used type of library resource on the Internet are online library catalogs. Of particular interest to architecture librarians are the catalogs of Columbia University, Harvard, Yale, Arizona State, University of California,

and the Library of Congress. There are many more of course. To obtain the telnet address and logon procedures for these and other libraries, access the list maintained at Yale, which is searchable by location or keyword. (Address: gopher yaleinfo.yale.edu/ Browse YaleInfo/ Library Catalogs World-Wide; URL: gopher://yaleinfo.yale.edu:7700/11/Internet LibraryCats).

Indexes and special databases such as the following are available through the Internet:

• The ACM SIGGRAPH Online Bibliography Project, searchable by key word, turns up material on such topics as CAD and computer graphics. It is available at several gophers, including UCSB's. Address: gopher ucsbuxa.ucsb.edu/ucsb gopher central/ Infosurf (Davidson Library Gopher)/ Subject Collections/ the Arts Collections/ Art and Architecture; URL: gopher://ucsbuxa.ucsb.edu:3001/11/.Arts/.Art.

• Arizona State's Solar Energy Index covers journal articles, patents, technical reports, pamphlets—on alternative energy sources. Address: telnet csi.carl.org/ Other Library Systems/Carl Corporation Network Libraries—Western US (Menu 1)/Arizona Libraries/ Other ASU Libraries Specialized Collections and Databases.

• Uncover should need no introduction by now! Address: telnet database.carl.org/Uncover.

• Archpics is an index to architectural illustrations provided by Carnegie Mellon. Address: telnet library.cmu.edu, login:library (press the esc key and 2 at the same time to change databases and get to archpics).

• The National Register of Historic Places is accessible through the University of Maryland. Entries include building name, location, date listed, geographical area, and National Register number. Address: telnet victor.umd.edu/ pac/vt100/other databases.

Gopher and web sites contributed by libraries and librarians, whether selected links to other sites or library guides and bibliographies, make excellent additions to your net bookmarks.

• The University of California Berkeley Library Gopher includes several library guides produced for the patrons of the UC-B Environmental Design Library, e.g. guides to architecture plans, book review sources, reference sources, and finding a job. There are also links to online archives of Cadalyst and Computer World Magazine, and other architecture information. Address: gopher infolib.lib.berkeley.edu/Research Databases and Resources by Subject/Architecture; URL: gopher://infolib.lib.berkeley.edu:70/11/resdbs/ arch

• Leininger's Home Page is created by MIT's Architecture Librarian, Michael Leininger, and provides guides, some annotated, to library information in architecture and construction, including guides to construction dictionaries, biographical sources, directories, building codes, accessibility information, and Boston architecture. URL:http://www.mit.edu:8001/afs/athena.mit.edu/user/m/j/mjl/www/pageone.html

• ArtSource provides text of bibliographies and guides, an archive of ARLIS-L discussions, and links to information on art and architecture (although it is much more heavily art than architecture). URL: http://www.uky.edu/Artsource/artsourcehome.html. Items are available for ftp from ftp://convex.cc.uky.edu/pub/artsource

• The Imagelib Clearinghouse lists library image database projects by institution and by media. Address: gopher dizzy.library.arizona.edu/ Image Databases/Clearinghouse of Image Databases in Libraries; URL: gopher://dizzy.library.arizona.edu:72/11/clearinghouse

• The University of Waterloo Library gopher's architecture offerings feature two interesting sections: "Quick Facts and Bibliographies in Architecture" which includes two bibliographies: Library Reference Materials in Architecture, and Library Resources on Architecture Schools and Practices; and "Doing Research in Architecture" which has guides like Architecture: How to Find Journal Articles, as well as other more general guides like How to Find a Book Review. Address: gopher watserv2.uwaterloo.ca/facilities/Library/finding/resources by discipline/architecture; URL: gopher://watserv2.uwaterloo.ca:70/00/facilities/University%20of%20Waterloo%20Library/finding/discipline/Architecture

University Architecture Programs
Many architecture programs are posting information on the Net. Some of the information is the standard sort found in college catalogs: information on staff, courses, and facilities. Some of the material provided goes far beyond: galleries of student work, tutorials, and images and descriptions of local architecture. Just a few of the schools with a net presence are listed here: School of Architecture Property and Planning, Auckland, New Zealand (URL: http://archpropplan.auckland.ac.nz); University of Miami School ofArchitecture (URL: http://rossi.arc.miami.edu); South Bank University Department of Architecture & Civil Engineering (URL: http://www.sbu.ac.uk/Architecture/home.html); Harvard Graduate School of Design (URL: http://gsd.harvard.edu/GSD.html); Mississippi State University School of Architecture (URL: http://wright.sarc.msstate.edu); and Curtin University of Technology, Perth, Australia, School of Architecture, Construction and Planning (URL: http://puffin.curtin.edu.au).

Images
Images are available at many of the gopher and web sites on the net.
There are some sites which are, however, primarily images.
• ArtServe, a web site of the Australian National University Institute of
the Arts (URL: http://rubens.anu.edu.au), has posted 2500 images of
classical architecture of the Mediterranean Basin and a survey of Islamic
architecture, and plans to add as many as 3000 images of European
sculpture and architecture from classical to 19th century. To go directly
to the searchable architecture database, use the URL: http://
rubens.anu.edu.au/architecture_form.html.
• The University of Virginia Digital Image Center, Fiske Kimball Fine
Arts Library (URL: http://www.lib.virginia.edu/dic/colls/arh102/
index.html) provides images from an architecture history class, on Re-
naissance and Baroque architecture in France and Italy.
• Images are posted to the newsgroups alt.binaries.pictures.fine-
art.graphics (for pictures done using computer graphics programs) and
alt.binaries.pictures.fine-art.digitized (for reproductions). Archives are
available for ftp (URL: ftp://uxa.ecn.bgu.edu/pub/fine-art).
• ArchiGopher (gopher libra.arch.umich.edu) features samples of
Palladio's architectural projects, CAD images, lunar architecture, and
Greek architecture.
• Spiro, the University of California Berkeley image library, has approximately 8000 images. To access it, you must have x windows.
Xhost pflueger.ced.berkeley.edu. Then telnet or rlogin to pflueger.
ced.berkeley
.edu. At the prompt, enter "netspiro". You will be prompted for the
name of your X Window display. Enter in the format: your.machine.
full.address:0. For additional information, and access through the web
go to URL: http://www.mip.berkeley.edu/mip/collections/arcslide.html

Discussions (Listservs and Newsgroups)
• DESIGN-L: this discussion group interprets "design" broadly to include arts, architecture, industrial design, etc. The list owner pulls many
postings from other discussion groups (like ARTCRIT) and newsgroups
(like alt.architecture). To subscribe send the subscription request to
listserv@psuvm or listserv@psuvm.psu.edu.
• Computer-related lists include AUTOCAD@jhuvm.hcf.jhu.edu, VTCAD-
L@vtvm2.bitnet (or @vtvm2.cc.vt.edu), Ingr-en (subscribe to this
Intergraph list by sending mail to mailserv@ccsun.tuke.sk), radiance-
discuss (send subscription message to radiance- request@hobbes.lbl.gov)
and GIF-L@itesmvf1.bitnet. There are others.

• The Consortium of Art and Architecture Historians (CAAH) is a restricted list. To apply send a subscribe message to listserv@pucc.bitnet or listserv@pucc.princeton.edu. You'll be given further instructions by email.

Several building/construction discussion groups are operating out of the UK:

• To subscribe to BUILT-ENVIRONMENT, BEPAC (Building Environmental Performance Analysis Club), IBPSA (International Building Performance Simulation Association), or IT-RD send a JOIN message (e.g. JOIN IT-RD First Name Last Name) to mailbase@mailbase.ac.uk. To browse the archives of mailbase lists, gopher to nisp.ncl.ac.uk (URL: gopher://nisp.ncl.ac.uk:70). Lists are in sections, alphabetically by list name.

• Cooperative Network for Building Researchers (CNBR-L). To join, send a message to edwards@rmit.edu.au with your name, department, institution; email, fax, phone and postal addresses; and indicate your main teaching and research areas. Not a discussion group, this list's mission is to circulate research enquiries and distribute information of common interest.

• The mailing list for the International Council for Building Research Studies and Documentation (CIB) Working Group 78 (W78) aims to "encourage and promote research and development in the application of integrated IT throughout the life-cycle of buildings and related facilities." To subscribe send the message sub w78.itcon to maiser@fagg.uni-lj.si. The archive of the list is at http://www.fagg.uni-lj.si/ICARIS/w78

• Also aimed at the building/construction side are ICARIS (to subscribe send message to mailserv@fagg.uni-lj.si. The message should read SUBSCRIBE ICARIS-L [Your Name]) and IRMA (to subscribe send mail to listserv@jhunix. hcf.jhu.edu with SUBSCRIBE IRMA-L [Your Name] in the body of the message).

• There are two lists particularly of interest to landscape architects: LARCH-L (send subscribe message to listserv@suvm.acs.syr.edu) and LARCHNET (subscribe to listserv@vm.uoguelph.ca). LARCH-L has substantially more postings than LARCHNET.

• Architecture librarians have several discussion groups. Two in the United States are ARLIS-L (listserv@ukcc.uky.edu), sponsored by Art Libraries Society of North America and AASL-L (listserv@unllib.unl.edu), sponsored by the Association of Architecture School Librarians. ARLIS-L has substantially more postings than AASL-L, but many of those are art rather than architecture related. Also of interest to Architecture Librarians is the listserv for users or potential users of the Art and Architecture Thesaurus. To subscribe to AAT-L, send the subscribe message to listserv@uicvm.cc.uic.edu.

• Image databases and conversions from non-digital formats to digital are some of the topics of IMAGELIB (listserv@listserv.arizona.edu).

There are several newsgroups relating to architecture, including alt.architecture. Some topics which have been discussed in the past on this newsgroup are architecture schools, alternatives to fiberglass insulation, pedestrian malls, and gargoyles. Other usenet newsgroups of interest are alt.housing.nontraditional, alt.architecture.alternative, alt.architecture.int-design, alt.cad, alt.planning.urban, sci.engr.lighting, misc.consumers.house, alt.landscape.architecture, and comp.cad.autocad. To browse through the various newsgroups, go to the gopher at the Virginia Polytechnic (Address: gopher gopher.vt.edu/other information services/ usenet news servers; URL: gopher://gopher.vt.edu:70/11/other/newsservers) which accesses a number of usenet news servers, including their own. Or access your own system's local news feed and reader (such as RN, TIN, or Trumpet).

Electronic Journals and Newsletters
One of the listings that has continued in existence since the April 1993 list is Architronic. It is still the only electronic journal in architecture! You can subscribe to Architronic, produced by the Kent State University Department of Architecture and Environmental Design, by sending a message to listserv@ kentvm.kent.edu : subscribe arcitron <name>. Various sites have different issues of Architronic. For the most recent issue go to URL:http:// www.kent.edu/Architronic/homepage.html. The Architronic archives is at URL: ftp://zeus.kent.edu (login: architecture; password: archives).

New, however, are several newsletters in the field. Energy Smart Newsletter aims to educate the consumer about energy efficient technology. It is also interesting for its orientation toward the incorporation of new communications technologies in buildings. The newsletter is available for ftp from marlin.gulf.net (cd/pub/esc). To subscribe, send your email address to Barry Goodwin at barryg16@aol.com or 4escinfo@gulf.net. GreenClips is a second newsletter. It is "a summary of recent articles in the media on environmental news. It has a special focus on sustainable design for buildings-green architecture-and related government and business issues. The one-page digital summary is published every two weeks." Address: gopher gopher.econet.apc.org/ Publications and News Services.

The Commerce Business Daily is accessible at gopher usic.savvy.com. This site provides free access to the last two weeks of CBD. To access the last year of CBD, and to store search profiles and automatically mail or ftp results costs $499 per year.

Accessibility and Universal Design
The Cornucopia of Disability Information contains the full-text of the Americans with Disabilities Act (ADA), as well as accessibility guidelines. Its address is gopher val-dor.cc.buffalo.edu/government documents.

The Adaptive Environments Universal Design Education Project is under construction but does have information on the education project and participants. From the menu structure, this site plans to provide universal design information by design discipline and by facility type. The address is gopher gopher.aces.k12.ct.us. The Universal Design Information Network operates a discussion list as well as a gopher. To subscribe send a message containing the word subscribe and your Internet address to udep-info-request@umbsky.cc.umb.edu.

Last Words
Architecture has been slow, compared to some disciplines, to develop substantial Internet resource sites. With the advent of graphical browsers—such as mosaic—interest and activity has intensified. Not only is the number of architecture-related sites increasing, but their content is becoming more creative and exciting!

Reprinted from C&RL News, *Vol. 54, No. 4, April 1993. Revised January 1995.*

Internet resources for Latin American studies

Molly Molloy

Since my first attempts to compile a guide to Latin American resources on the Internet in May 1993, the quantity of information products and modes of access has exploded. It is no longer possible to know all, or list all resources; the best alternative is to point the new researcher to the best compilations and information servers now available in the Latin America "region" of the Net.

The librarians' tendency to think in terms of genre (encyclopedias, handbooks, atlases, etc.) has carried over into Internet guides where the genres used (Gophers, WWW pages, FTP archives, WAIS indexes) actually describe software tools or network services that enable the user to access the same universe of electronic information products stored in millions of files on computers all over the world connected to the Internet. In some cases the same information product will be accessible in multiple ways, depending on the tools available to the user.

The first part of this introductory guide will point to specific information products and/or places that serve as gateways into the vast array of Latin American resources on the net. The second part will mention a few of the hundreds of electronic conferences, email lists and newsgroups devoted to Latin America-related topics. A few carefully picked list subscriptions can be the best way to obtain information about new resources as they become available.

Molly Molloy is reference librarian, social sciences/Latin American studies at New Mexico State University Library, Las Cruces; e-mail: mmolloy@nmsu.edu.

PART 1
Information Product and Gateways

Most of these resources are accessible via gopher, WWW, or both. WWW servers offer a hypertext interface to information and allow the display and retrieval of graphics, sound and other media. Gopher provides access to text documents through a system of menus. Some information products may be available through numerous servers; once a document is posted on the net, other servers can link to it.

• LATIN AMERICAN STUDIES MAIL LISTS & CONFERENCES, compiled by Gladys Smiley Bell, included in the 9th Revision of the Directory of Scholarly Electronic Conferences, edited by Diane Kovacs and the Directory Team, Kent State University, 1995.

The most current version of this guide can be found in the University of Michigan Subject-Oriented Guides to the Internet.

• URL:gopher://una.hh.lib.umich.edu:70/00/inetdirsstacks/acadlist.latam

An excellent list of academic electronic mail conferences relating to Latin America.

• INTERNET RESOURCES FOR LATIN AMERICA, compiled by Molly Molloy. URL: gopher://lib.nmsu.edu:70/00/.subjects/.border/.lanet

This guide is a longer version of the material presented here. The guide is updated regularly and (like the Internet) should never be considered static or published or finished. The most current versions of this guide (last revision 9/94) is kept in the NMSU Library gopher, LANIC and the University of Michigan Subject Oriented Guides to the Internet.

• NEW MEXICO STATE UNIVERSITY LIBRARY GOPHER/RESOURCES BY SUBJECT/BORDER & LATIN AMERICAN INFORMATION. URL: gopher://lib.nmsu.edu:70/11/.subjects/.border

This subdirectory provides links to most of the resources mentioned in this article, information about the subscription service—Latin America Data Base, several public access electronic journals relating to the border or Latin America; postings of news from Internet sources relating to the US-Mexico border and Mexico from August 1994—.

• UT-LANIC: LATIN AMERICAN NETWORK INFORMATION CENTER (gopher & World Wide Web). URL: gopher://lanic.utexas.edu:70/0/0/ URL: http://lanic.utexas.edu/

For users without gopher or WWW clients LANIC can also be accessed via email and telnet:

Email: gopher@lanic.utexas.edu

Telnet: (VT100): lanic.utexas.edu (login: lanic)

This information system provided by the University of Texas Institute of Latin American Studies provides the most comprehensive gateway to Latin

American information on the Internet. LANIC provides access to library catalogs, specialized databases, internet access tools and information, FTP archives, economic/social statistics from Latin America, links to most internet
sites in all Latin American countries. The WWW page contains maps for
most countries and other graphical sources—most from the University of
Texas Benson Latin American Collection. For more information contact
<info@lanic.utexas.edu>
• RED CIENTIFICA PERUANA—RCP (Peruvian Scientific Network) Access
via gopher and World Wide Web. URL: gopher://chasqui.rcp.net.pe:70/ URL:
http://www.rcp.net.pe/
RCP provides an excellent gateway to the Internet from South America. It
includes many useful internet documents and instructional tools in Spanish. RCP maintains a directory of Latin American Networks that can be useful to identify providers in almost every country. The server contains much
information about Peru, news services, and gateways to other servers and
libraries in South America. RCP maintains discussion groups on a variety of
topics. Director: Jose Soriano <js@rcp.net.pe>
CHICANO/LATINONET. URL: gopher://latino.sscnet.ucla.edu:70/
Clearinghouse for information on Chicano/Latino research at the University
of California and elsewhere. Produced by the Chicano Studies Research
Center, UCLA. Director: Richard Chabran <chabran@latino.sscnet.ucla.edu>
• USAID LATIN AMERICAN & CARIBBEAN ECONOMIC & SOCIAL DATA
URL: gopher://lanic.utexas.edu:70/11/la/region/aid
Access to this data is via UT-LANIC. In the UT-LANIC menu system it is
located at Latin America/Latin America General Information/Latin America
and the Caribbean/Economic and Social Data, USAID. Excellent source for
current statistics covering many economic and social indicators including
education, environment, health, poverty, trade, etc. It is easy to find charts
with specific information and to download or email.
• LA JORNADA (Mexican newspaper via WWW). URL: http://www.sccs.
swarthmore.edu:80/~justin/jornada/index.html
This independent Mexican newspaper appeared on the WWW in February
1995. Current editions of the paper are available with text and graphics,
providing instant coverage of news events in Mexico.
• MEXICAN NEWSPAPERS VIA FTP. [binary image files] Provided by the
Universidad Autonoma de Mexico.
To retrieve these files FTP to <condor.dgsca.unam.mx> and go to the <pub/
imagen/noticia/periodicos> directory. At this point, use a <dir> or <ls -al>
command to see a list of the newspapers. The list includes: El Economista,
El Nacional, Excelsior, La Jornada, Sintesis, and Uno mas Uno.
This FTP archive contains scanned images of the pages of these newspapers

on a daily basis. The resulting files are very large, compressed, binary image files which can be transferred via FTP and must be uncompressed before they are usable. You must also have a graphics filter that makes it possible to view files with a .tif extension.

PART 2:
Electronic Mail Groups & Usenet Newsgroups

Most of the lists mentioned below use the listserv software. Subscribe automatically by addressing a message to <listserv@whatever.where.edu>. The body of the message should be <subscribe something-l your name>. Some lists do not use listserv and you must send a message to an address, perhaps <listname-request@something.somewhere.org> asking to subscribe. You will also see other list software such as <majordomo> and <listproc>. Each of these has slightly different protocols for subscribing and unsubscribing to lists. For detailed information on list commands address a message to the listserv, listproc, or majordomo address with the single word <help> in the body of the message. You will receive a return mail message with the information you need.

I have tried to provide the most current information available for the lists, but addresses change and lists come and go. Any listserv site will provide detailed instructions on interacting with the listserv software. Also, upon subscribing to a list, you will receive a message with basic information on the purpose, membership rules (if any) and other necessary information. Not all lists are available for open subscription. If this is the case, your listserv request to subscribe will be forwarded to a list moderator who will either sign you up, or inform you of rules for list subscription.

The following list is only a very small sample of what is available.

• ACTIV-L: Peace, Democracy, Freedom, Justice (Activists' Mailing List) To subscribe send message to <listserv@mizzou1.missouri.edu> To send messages to the list <activ-l@mizzou1.missouri.edu>. This list also exists on USENET as <misc.activism.progressive>.
This is a very busy list covering all kinds of progressive/radical political issues. Of interest to Latin Americanists because many activist/human rights groups post news and bulletins from numerous Latin American countries. Excellent source for news from El Salvador, Guatemala, Haiti, Peru and other countries. Also postings from environmental, trade, development organizations.

• CHIAPAS-L: Chiapas Discussion. To subscribe send a message to <majordomo@profmexis.dgsca.unam.mx> Post messages to <chiapas-l@profmexis.dgsca.unam.mx> For more information contact the list owner, Arturo Grunstein <grunst@profmexis.dgsca.unam.mx>.

An open, unmoderated discussion concerning the conflict in the state of Chiapas. Languages Spanish and English. Postings from various news services appear on this list daily.

• CUBA-L: Cuba Today. To subscribe send message to <listserv@unmvma. unm.edu>. Moderator: Nelson Valdes <nvaldes@bootes.unm.edu>.
News on current events in Cuba from many sources including wire services, Radio Havana Cuba and the Voice of America.

• EC-NOTICIAS-L: Ecuador News Bulletins "Diario Hoy" To subscribe send message to <listproc@lac.net> Do not post to the list. Questions may be addressed to Luis Fierro <lfierro@mundo.eco.utexas.edu>.
Excellent source for news from Ecuador. Daily news bulletins from "Diario Hoy" include Ecuador news and also important news from elsewhere in the region.

• ELAN—The Environment in Latin America Network: To subscribe send a message to listproc@csf.colorado.edu>. To post: <elan@csf.colorado.edu>
ELAN was established in July 1994 by the Environment and Natural Resources Working Group of the Latin American Studies Association for the purpose of providing communications links between researchers, activists and others with an interest in environmental issues in Latin America. Listowner: Timmons Roberts <timmons@mailhost.tcs.tulane.edu>. The list will be archived in the environment directory of the Center for a Sustainable Future gopher at <csf.colorado.edu>.

• LADIG-L: Latin American Database Interest Group. To subscribe send message to <listserv@unmvma.unm.edu>. Roma Arellano <ladbad@bootes. unm.edu>.
Announcements and discussion of database products and services from and about Latin America.

• LALA-L: Latin Americanist Librarians' Announcements List. To subscribe <listserv@uga.cc.uga.edu>. Messages to <lala-l@uga.cc.uga.edu> Moderator: Gayle Williams <gwilliam@uga.cc.uga.edu>
Announcements and discussion for Latin American Studies librarians and others. Currently restricted to members of the Seminar on the Acquisition of Latin American Library Materials (SALALM).

• LASNET: Latin American Studies Network. To subscribe send a message to: <listproc@mcfeeley.utexas.edu>. Post messages to <lasnet@mcfeeley .cc.utexas.edu>
LASNET is an unmoderated list with over 600 subscribers for the purpose of facilitating communication among Latin Americanists internationally. Contains announcements of new net resources, publications, conferences, etc. For more information contact Kent Norsworthy at <lasnet-request@uts.cc. utexas.edu>.

• LATCO: Business & Trade with Latin America. Latin American Trade Council of Oregon. To subscribe send a message to <lserv@psg.com> To post messages to the list <latco@psg.com> Produced by the Latin American Trade Council of Oregon. Moderator: Tom Miles <tmiles@well.sf.ca.us.

Discussion list for trade and economic data, analysis, opinions and experience, sources of information about Latin American business and industry, conference announcements, etc.

• MCLR-L: Midwest Consortium for Latino Research. To subscribe <listserv@msu.edu> Post to <mclr-l@msu.edu>

Dialogue among Latino scholars and others in the United States. Announcement of grants available, academic jobs of interest to Latinos and other in formation and discussion.

• MEXICO94: To subscribe send a message to <majordomo@profmexis. dgsca.unam.mx> Post messages to <mexico94@profmexis.dgsca.unam.mx>. of the message.

List established in April 1994 to discuss the political transitions in Mexico— rebellion, assassination, elections. Contact: Arturo Grunstein <grunst@profmexis.dgsca.unam.mx>

• NATIVE-L: Indigenous Peoples Information; NAT-LANG: Languages of Indigenous Peoples; NATCHAT: Indigenous Peoples Discussion. Three separate lists available for subscription via <listserv@tamvm1.tamu.edu> Post messages to <native-l@tamvm1.tamu.edu> <natch at@tamvm1.tamu.edu> <nat-lang@tamvm1.tamu.edu>

These lists deal with various issues related to indigenous peoples worldwide. Politics, culture, information sources are all discussed. Participants include academics, activists, students, etc. Good news source for information on environment, human rights, politics, etc. in Latin America, especially for Guatemala, Brazil, Ecuador, Peru and other countries with large indigenous populations. Archive maintained at <listserv@tamvm1.tamu.edu>. Parallel USENET groups<alt.native> and <soc.culture.native>

• NEW-LIST: Announcements of new bitnet/internet mailing lists. Not specifically Latin America related, but NEW-LIST is a good list to subscribe to for general updates. To subscribe send message to <listserv@ndsuvm1.nodak. edu>. NEW-LIST announces newly established e-mail lists on bitnet and internet. The <listserv@vm1.nodak.edu> also provides a good database to search for the existence of lists by keywords. To perform a search send the following database commands to <listserv@vm1.nodak.edu>

```
//dblook job echo=no
database search dd=rules
//rules  dd *
select searchterm in lists
```

index
select searchterm in intgroup
index
select searchterm in new-list
index
    The listserv will search bitnet, internet and new-list archives lists of lists
for mailing lists that contain your searchterm. By return email you will receive a list of results.

Usenet News From & About Latin America
The following USENET newsgroups concern Latin America, Latinos in the
U.S. and other parts of the world, and other Hispanic regions of the world:
- soc.culture.latin-america
- soc.culture.mexican
- soc.culture.mexican-american
- soc.culture.caribbean
- alt.culture.argentina
- soc.culture.argentina
- soc.culture.portuguese
- soc.culture.spain
- soc.culture.peru
- soc.culture.brazil
- soc.culture.argentina
- soc.culture.uruguay
- soc.culture.chile
- soc.culture.venezuela
- alt.current-events.haiti
- alt.culture.us.southwest
- rec.music.afro-latin
- soc.culture.puerto-rico
- soc.culture.ecuador
- soc.culture.cuba

    To read USENET news you must have access via a news reader on your
local system or through access to another system. Find out about local access by contacting your computer center or other internet access provider.
For example, the Peacenet and other IGC networks provide access to Usenet
News.

    These newsgroups discuss almost anything relating to society, politics,
travel, culture, etc. for the regions described. The groups sometimes include
postings from newspapers and wire services. Various languages, mostly
Spanish, Portuguese, English. Much info is cross-posted to other lists. USENET

groups often have a regular posting called an FAQ (frequently asked questions) that provides a lot of good information about the content and culture of the list and will usually let you know if you want to be come a regular participant.

USENET groups can be created by a voting process and they can also disappear for lack of interest. Numbers of messages posted range from 1 to 1000+ in the groups mentioned above. Why <alt>, why <soc>? The USENET hierarchy has developed over the years as a way to group certain categories of newsgroups together. <soc> generally means something devoted to discussion of society and culture. <alt> is the "alternative" hierarchy within Usenet and generally means a group with less rules and more open discussion and tolerance for weirdness. <rec> generally refers to hobby-related groups. If you participate in the USENET community, it will all become clear.

Reprinted from C&RL News, *Vol. 54, No. 7, July/August 1993. Revised January 1995.*

Internet for Russian and East European studies

Michael Markiw

Wherever possible, information has been provided to update the original article, published September 1993 in *College and Research Libraries News*. Some closed computer conferences have been identified and similar conferences are suggested. Information on closed conferences has been retained, since their archives may still be accessible. The enhanced navigational capabilities of some World Wide Web browsers have aroused intense interest in the Web as a means of Internet access. Therefore, some recently established Web sites focusing on Russian and East European Studies are listed below. They are recommended as excellent starting points for study of this area. The original article was intended to present a selective listing of Internet resources for Russian and East European studies. Despite the addition of some new information, space considerations again dictate the need for selective listings.

The continually expanding Internet, a group of interconnected computer networks, links educational, government and commercial organizations worldwide. Perhaps the largest computer network in the world, its considerable size contributes to a vast pool of information. Much of it is so disorganized, however, one often resorts to discovering information by "net surfing" via navigational tools such as World Wide Web browsers. In order to further systematize information within the Internet, efforts are underway to organize some of it by subject. One result of these efforts is this selected

Michael Markiw is slavic studies librarian at Arizona State University, Tempe; e-mail: iemxm@asuacad.bitnet, or iemxm@asuvm.inre.asu.edu

listing of Internet resources for Russian and East European studies consisting of computer conferences of special interest groups, electronic journals, newsletters and online bibliographies.

Computer Conferences

Subscriptions to listservs provide access to computer conferences of special interest groups. Listserv groups may have Internet or Bitnet addresses, for example, POLAND-L@UBVM.CC.BUFFALO.EDU (Internet) and POLAND-L@UBVM (Bitnet). Subscribers with Internet addresses should use the listserv's Internet address (e.g., LISTSERV@UBVM.CC.BUFFALO.EDU) and subscribers with Bitnet addresses should use the listserv's Bitnet address (e.g., LISTSERV@UBVM). After the subscription has been requested, the subscriber will receive confirmation and further participation instructions. Other conferences appear as newsgroups on Usenet, a large international computer network which provides access through most university campus computer systems. Below is a selective list of conferences.

• BALT-INFO links librarians and information specialists in major research libraries of Estonia, Latvia and Lithuania with their counterparts in the West. Initially, this new network intends to provide information exchange among librarians about Baltic-related library resources and serve as an electronic information resource on the Baltic area. Eventually, other interested researchers in the field of Baltic studies will be able to receive help with bibliographical citations as well as submit reference requests. For subscription information contact Dawn Mann at MANND@RFERL.ORG.

• BALT-L@UBVM (Baltic Republics Discussion List) discusses politics and current affairs of Estonia, Latvia and Lithuania.

• EOCHR (Eastern Orthodox Christian Discussion List) provides a forum for exchange of ideas among members of Eastern and Orthodox churches around the world and other individuals interested in Eastern Orthodox Christianity. Contact Dragic V. Vukomanovic, DRAGIC.VUKOMANOVIC@QUEENSU.CA. for subscription information.

• EUEARN-L@UBVM (Discussion of Eastern Europe Telecommunications) is concerned with computer communications and technology within this region.

• E-EUROPE@PUCC or E-EUROPE@PUCC.PRINCETON.EDU (The Eastern Europe Business Network List) discusses business and economic systems of Central and Eastern Europe and the Commonwealth of Independent States.

• HUNGARY@GWUVM (Hungarian Discussion List) provides information on Hungary and Hungarian issues.

• INFO-RUSS serves as an informational medium for members of the Russian emigre community in the U.S., Canada, Israel, Europe, Australia, South

Africa and other countries. Contact Alexander Kaplan, SASHA@SUPER.ECE.JHU.EDU.

• MIDEUR-L@UBVM or MIDEUR-L@UBVM.CC.BUFFALO.EDU (Discussion of Middle Europe Topics) focuses on Central European politics, history and culture. Topics often relate to Eastern Europe.

• POLAND-L@UBVM, or, POLAND-L@UBVM.CC.BUFFALO.EDU provides a forum for discussion of Polish current events and culture. Contributions are in Polish and English.

• RUSHIST@UMRVMB or RUSHIST@CSEARN (Russian History Forum) discusses Russian history from 1462-1917.

• RUSSIA@ARIZVM1 or RUSSIA@ARIZVM1.CC.IT.ARIZONA.EDU (Russia and Her Neighbors List) was concerned with the new order within the former Soviet Union and political affairs of neighboring countries. This list closed effective December 1, 1993, approximately three months after the article was published. Archives of this conference, according to the former list owner, are not presently accessible on ARIZVM1 and are not online elsewhere at this time.

• RUSTEX-L@UBVM (Russia TeX and Cyrillic Processing List) focuses on representation of Cyrillic characters on computer screens. Covers Cyrillic text processing and transliteration of Slavic and non-Slavic Cyrillic alphabet languages.

• SCS-L@INDYCMS or newsgroup soc.culture.soviet dealt with cultural issues within the former Soviet Union. Both groups have been discontinued but archives are still available on INDYCMS.

• SEELANGS@CUNYVM or SEELANGS@VM.USC.EDU (Slavic and East European Languages and Literatures List) promotes scholarly communication among members of the American Association of Teachers of Slavic and East European Languages but includes nonmembers. Also features Russian satellite television program schedules.

• SLOVAK-L@UBVM or SLOVAK-L@UBVM.CC.BUFFALO.EDU (Discussion of Slovak issues) is concerned with politics and current events within the newly established Slovak Republic. An English translation of the entire Constitution of the Slovak Republic is available within the archives of this discussion group.

• SOVHIST@UMRVMB or SOVHIST@CSEARN (Soviet History Forum) covers Soviet History from 1917-1991.

• TPS-L@INDYCMS (Talk Politics Soviet) or newsgroup talk.politics.soviet focused on political and economic issues relating to Russia and other former Soviet republics. Both groups have been discontinued and their archives are not currently available on INDYCMS.

• UKRAINA@UKANAIX.CC.UKANS.EDU discusses university course topics, research, and books about Ukraine. Announcements of events in or about

Ukraine are also posted. The primary members of this network are students and faculty of the Russian and East European Studies program at the University of Kansas but associate memberships are extended to scholars and students of other academic institutions who have academic interests in Ukraine.

• UKRAINE@ARIZVM1 or UKRAINE@ARIZVM1.CCIT.ARIZONA.EDU was devoted to the exchange of information about Ukraine and included Ukrainian language, history, geography, churches and films. This list was closed effective December 1, 1993, approximately three months after the original article was published. Archives of this conference, according to the former list owner, are not presently accessible on ARIZVM1 and are not online anywhere else. The UKRAINA list, mentioned above, is suggested as an alternative.

• VAL-L@MARIST (Michael Valentine Smith's Commentary) discusses political and social issues within Russia, other former Soviet republics and Eastern Europe.

• Some newsgroups focusing on Eastern European countries or regions and available on Usenet include soc.culture.baltics, soc.culture.bosna-herzgvna, soc.culture.bulgaria, soc.culture.cis, soc.culture.croatia, soc.culture.czecho-slovak, soc.culture.magyar, soc.culture.europe, soc.culture.polish, soc.culture.romanian, soc.culture.ukrainian and soc.culture.yugoslavia.

Electronic Journals

Subscription requests for electronic journals are generally sent to either a listserv or to the individual responsible for its distribution.

• DONOSY offers daily news bulletins from Poland. Articles are in Polish but a weekly English language version is available. For U.S. subscriptions contact Przemek Klosowski, PRZEMEK@NDCVX.CC.ND.EDU; outside the U.S. send requests to DONOSY@PLEARN.

• RFERL-L (RFE/RL Daily Report), issued by the RFE/RL Research Institute, a division of Radio Free Europe/Radio Liberty Inc., is an excellent source of current events information on Russia, Transcaucasia, Central Asia, and Central and Eastern Europe. Each issue, published Monday through Friday, may present information on government meetings, parliamentary decisions, newly approved laws, trade-union activities, ethnic tensions, and troop movements within the above-mentioned areas. Reports are available via LISTSERV@UBVM.CC.BUFFALO.EDU or from LISTSERV@UBVM.

• SUEARN-L@UBVM (Connecting the USSR to the Internet Digest) or newsgroup bit.listserv.su-earn, provides information on telecommunication links within Eastern Europe. Articles may include directions for reaching

Russian and Eastern European sites by electronic mail, computer networks, databases, information technology, and the online industry within this area.

Newsletters

Subscription requests for newsletters are generally sent to the individual responsible for its distribution.

• CAROLINA@CSEARN, a weekly newsletter reporting on current events in the Czech Republic, is published by the students of journalism at Charles University in Prague. Articles are in Czech or English.

A number of newsletters describe current events in the countries comprising the former Yugoslavia.

• Bosnet, published daily, covers news of Bosnia and Herzegovina. Articles are mostly in English and languages spoken in Bosnia. Contact Hozo Iztok, HOZO@MATH.LSA.UMICH.EDU.

• Croatian-News (English)/Hrvatski-Vjesnik (Croatian) offers news from Croatia, Bosnia & Herzegovina and Slovenia. News sources may include transcripts from Croatian and other newspapers. Croatian-News is available from CROATIAN-NEWS-REQUEST@ANDREW.CMU.EDU and Hrvatski-Vjesnik can be obtained from HRVATSKI-VJESNIK-ZAMOLBE@ANDREW.CMU.EDU.

• MILS-NEWS, published by the Macedonian Information and Liaison Service, is a digest of current events in Macedonia. It is issued daily in English and Macedonian via listserver MAK-NEWS@UTS.EDU.AU.

• RokPress presents news from Slovenia. Slovene is the principal language, but news from Croatian and Serbian sources may be included. Subscriptions can be requested from Igor Benko, IBENKO@MAVERICO.UWATERLOO.CA.

• SII distributes news and discusses current events affecting Serbs. Contact OWNER@MOUMEE.CALSTATELA.EDU.

• VND (Vreme News Digest) is an electronic English language version of the weekly newspaper *Vreme,* which serves all areas of former Yugoslavia. Selected articles from *Vreme* are translated into English. For subscriptions contact Dmitrije Stamenovic, DIMITRIJE@BUENGA.BU.EDU.

Online Bibliographies

ABSEES Online, an electronic version of the *American Bibliography of Slavic and East European Studies* available at no charge via the Internet, is a source of citations for journal articles, government and research reports, book chapters, and books published in the United States and Canada. Contact Patt Leonard, Editor, *ABSEES,* absees@uxl.cso.uiuc.edu.

The World Wide Web

As mentioned above, the World Wide Web (WWW) has recently become extremely popular due to the emergence of browsers such as Mosaic, Netscape, and Lynx. Such browsers can access WWW sites which offer documents and online links to databases, libraries, and reference tools. REENIC (The Russian and East European Network Information Center), sponsored by The Center for Post-Soviet and East European Studies at The University of Texas in Austin, provides scholars of Eastern Europe and the former Soviet Union with such services. REENIC can be accessed via most WWW browsers by typing the following Universal Resource Locator (URL): http://reenic.utexas.edu/reenic/home.html. REESWeb (Russian and East European Studies Home Pages) is a collaborative effort by the University of Pittsburgh Center for Russian and East European Studies and the University of Pittsburgh Library System. The Pages serve as a guide to Web resources on Russia and Eastern Europe. Among the most interesting features on this Web site is the listing of national WWW home pages of countries within the former Soviet Union and Eastern Europe. REESWeb can be accessed on most Web browsers via the URL: http://www.pitt.edu/"cjp/rees.html. Both REENIC and REESWeb appear to strive for comprehensiveness and offer new resources as they become available. By monitoring these two sites, scholars of Russian and Eastern Europe can keep abreast of Internet developments in their area.

Reprinted from C&RL News, *Vol. 54, No. 8, September 1993. Revised January 1995.*

Internet resources for psychology

Paul Fehrmann

Users learn on a daily basis that the dynamism of the Internet can challenge efforts to find information, even as it provides expanding fruitful options. As noted in the April 1993 issue of *College & Research Libraries News*, however, working lists of resources related to subject areas have been viewed as potentially helpful for those using the Internet. And so, as one such listing, the material below is intended to give a beginning set of sources which can be used by researchers and students in psychology.

Brief information on Gopher and "World Wide Web" Internet systems, along with comments on subscribing to electronic journals and conferences, is given just below. Next, readers will find descriptions of resources, organized by kind of resource or kind of information, along with information for Telnet, Gopher, or World Wide Web access to the resources.

A major Internet system for sharing resources is the Gopher system, and users who have a Gopher "client" (and TCP/IP) software running on their personal computers (or local mainframes) can type in the addresses given below in order to "Gopher to" listed resources. The Gopher software has been freely available, but for "set up", first time users may wish to consult with computer systems staff or other experienced colleagues. Alternate (though limited) access to Gopher resources has also been available by telnetting to "public" sites (preferably at night or early morning); telnet to CONSULTANT.MICRO.UMN.EDU, or telnet to UX1.CSO.UIUC.EDU (login at

Paul Fehrmann is a librarian at Kent State University Libraries, Ohio; e-mail: pfehrman@kentvm.kent.edu

both sites as gopher). Accessing Gopher resources listed below at such "public" sites might involve "browsing" to connect to them (e.g., use public Gopher to find software reviews by finding SUNY at Plattsburgh directory under New York under USA under North America in the list of all Gophers, and then choose COMPSYCH). Additionally, Veronica, the index to Gopher which has been under "Other Gopher and Information Servers" at public sites, has been useful for keyword searches of and connection to Gopher menu resources. Again, use of this resource during "off hours" can be more productive; and, once connected, getting and reading documentation on how to search Veronica can be helpful.

Many resources are also available in the World Wide Web system, and readers using HTTP client software (e.g., Mosaic, Cello, Lynx, MacWeb, Netscape) will find HTTP resource addresses below. The software needed for this kind of access has also been freely available, and again, first time users may wish to consult with computer systems colleagues or other experienced colleagues. Gopher and Telnet resources can also be accessed using the HTTP clients. Additionally, like Veronica for Gopher, there are keyword searching tools developed which result in lists of resources to which you can connect. For connections to a number of such tools, use http://webcrawler.cs.washington.edu/WebCrawler/WebIndexes.html.

Another major set of "search engines" has been available at http://cui_www.unige.ch/meta-index.html. To begin to browse, a fairly large listing of Internet psychology resources has been at Stanford; use http://matia.stanford.edu/cogsci.html.

A standard procedure for subscribing to both electronic journals and to electronic conferences (lists) is given below; and these steps work for all conferences and journals noted here. Subscription procedures can vary, however, and directories can help (e.g., The Directory of Electronic Journals, Newsletters And Academic Discussion Lists, published by the Association of Research Libraries, 1995).

Library Catalogs
Internet library catalogs for select areas in psychology might be identified as follows: first identify schools where there might be strengths, using publications such as APA's Guide to Graduate Study in Psychology or the list of APA programs found each year in the American Psychologist; next, catalog access information can be found using Gopher. Gopher to LIBERTY. UC.WLU.EDU and, under Explore Internet Resources, find Telnet Login to Sites (Hytelnet); or Gopher to YALEINFO.YALE.EDU and under Browse YaleInfo Information find Library Catalogs Worldwide; or Gopher to GOPHER.MICRO.UMN.EDU and look under Libraries. Two other catalogs are

those of the Library of Congress (telnet to LOCIS.LOC.GOV) and the National Library of Medicine (telnet to LOCATOR.NLM.NIH.GOV; login as LOCATOR). The Library of Congress is also making resources available via the Gopher; Gopher to MARVEL.LOC.GOV.

Journals/Serials
A number of approaches have developed on the Internet for accessing material provided in journals.
• For paper journal table of contents information, telnet to DATABASE.CARL.ORG and choose to search the CARL "Uncover" database. A large selection of titles is available, including many psychology journals. Browse current table of contents, or set up a profile to have such contents from titles you choose automatically emailed to you when available. The possibility of ordering fulltext has also been available at this site.
• Paper journals have themselves also offered products. The site for The Journal of Applied Behavioral Analysis and the Journal of the Experimental Analysis of Behavior has provided keyword searching resulting in citations and abstracts from these titles; use http://www.envmed.rochester.edu/wwwrap/behavior/JEABJABA2.HTM. For Behavioral and Brain Sciences journal information and target article reprints, use http://www.princeton.edu/~harnad/bbs.html. For Journal of Cognitive Neuroscience or Cerebral Cortex journal and article information, use http://neuroscience.ucdavis.edu/JOCN/JOCN.html.
• A number of electronic journals have been available in psychology. The three journals below are peer reviewed.
    • Psycoloquy; all areas of Psychology (Psyc@PUCC)
    • Psychology Graduate Student Journal (Psygrd-J@UOTTAWA)
    • Psyche; Consciousness (Psyche-L@NKI)
To subscribe to Psycoloquy, as an example: 1) I would address e-mail to this address, LISTSERV@PUCC.BITNET; 2) I would not put anything in the name field when asked; 3) I would also leave the e-mail subject field blank; and 4) I would then send this message SUBSCRIBE PSYC Paul Fehrmann
• To browse archives of electronic serials, gopher to GOPHER.CIC.NET; and then choose Electronic Serials. Next, for example, by choosing the alphabetical listing, and looking under "p", you can find and browse or retrieve issues of Psycoloquy or Psycgrad, or Psyche. HTTP access for issues of electronic journal archives has also been available. For Psycoloquy, use http://www.princeton.edu/~harnad/psyc.html. For Psyche, use http://hcrl.open.ac.uk/psyche/psyche.html.
Another title, the Practical Psychology Magazine, has offered practical articles written by mental health professionals; use http://www.thegroup.net/ppm/ppmhome.htm.

Electronic Conferences

Dialogue, debate, and collaboration have emerged as widespread activities on the Internet, and the conferences listed below are a sampling of over 30 in psychology which are currently active. To subscribe to the electronic conferences listed below, follow the sample shown above for subscribing to electronic journals. Subscription to other conferences can vary, and directions are found in the ARL publication noted above as well as in the noted just below.

- AUTISM@SJUVM (Developmental Disabilities)
- BEHAVIOR@ASUACAD (Behavior Disorders in Children/Youth)
- ADDICT-L@KENTVM (Addictions other than Alcohol/Drugs)
- MPSYCH-L@BROWNVM (Mathematical Psychology)
- DIV28@GWUVM (APA's Div 28; Psychopharmacology)

• Directories. To help find conferences which focus on a particular topic, an annotated list of psychology-related conferences (including descriptions and subscription information) has been available for browsing or keyword searching at the following two sites. With Gopher, use GOPHER.USASK.CA, look under Computing and find the Directory of Scholarly Electronic Conferences. For HTTP access, use http://www.mid.net/KOVACS/; browse the directory structure or choose from several keyword search options. Alternatively, the Clearinghouse for Subject-Oriented Internet Resource Guides, at the University of Michigan, has provided guides including this conference information. Gopher to UNA.HH.LIB.UMICH.EDU and, under INETDIRS, find Guides on the Social Sciences, and then look for Psychology & Psychiatry; or use http://www.lib.umich.edu/chhome.html and look under Social Sciences. Related guides (e.g., for Neuroscience and Philosophy) have also been available at the Michigan site, and all can be retrieved as text files.

• InterPsych. This international organization has been providing interdisciplinary forums (electronic conferences) in a variety of topical areas related to psychopathology. For information contact Ian Pitchford, using I.Pitchford@SHEFFIELD.AC.UK.

• RedePsi. With the main language of Spanish or Portuguese (though English is also used), this service has supported collaboration and discussion (electronic conferences, etc.) for Latin American professionals in a number of areas of psychology. For information, contact Cesar Piccinini, using RedePsi@VORTEX.UFRGS.BR.

• Psychology and Support Groups Pointer. For a list of Usenet newsgroups and topics they typically cover, use http://www.cis.ohio- state.edu/hypertext/faq/usenet/finding-groups/psychology-and- support/faq.html.

Tests, Measurements, and Behavior Analysis
• For access to keyword searching which results in citations to or information from Buros Test Reviews, Educational Testing Service files, or Test Critiques from Pro-Ed, Gopher to VMSGOPHER.CUA.EDU and look under Special Resources, and then under ERIC Clearinghouse, find Test Locator.
• Sites for Behavioral Analysis include the following: Gopher to ALPHA1.CSD.UWM.EDU and look under UWM Information, and then under Psychology. To connect to one of several other relevant sites, use http://www.coedu.usf.edu/behavior/behavior.html.
• The Journal of Applied Behavior Analysis and the Journal of the Experimental Analysis of Behavior are two related resources. Use http://www.envmed.rochester.edu/wwwrap/behavior/JEABJABA2.HTM GRANTS AND FUNDING IN PSYCHOLOGY.
• Abstracts of NSF Grant Awards in psychology (from 1990). Gopher to STIS.NSF.GOV; do a keyword search on psychology after choosing the Index to NSF Award Abstracts.
• Announcements of Grants/Funding in psychology. Subscribe to APASD-L; subscription address is LISTSERV@VTVM2.

Software and Computer Use for Psychology Research
The first two selections below have browseable/retrievable archives. They have served as official archives pertaining to software discussed in the Psychonomic Society's journal Behavior Research Methods, Instruments, & Computers.
• For PC-Based Psychology Software, gopher to BARYON.HAWK.PLATTS-BURGH.EDU; choose COMPSYCH.
• For Psychology Research with the Macintosh, gopher to GOPHER.STOLAF.EDU, under Network Resources, then under St. Olaf Mailing Lists, find MacPsych.
• Discussion of Experiment Generator Packages. Subscribe to PSYCH-EXPTS; send e-mail to MAILBASE@MAILBASE.AC.UK; message=join psych-expts yourFirstname yourLastname

Datafiles
• For Inter-university Consortium for Political and Social Research Datafiles/Information, gopher to GOPHER.ICPSR.UMICH.EDU, or to DATALIB.LIBRARY.UALBERTA.CA.
• For Social Science Data/Archive Information, telnet to HAR1.HUJI.AC.IL; login as SSDA; choose Online Aleph.
• For Institute for Research in Social Science Information, gopher to GIBBS.OIT.UNC.EDU and look in Research selection; or, using http://

www.unc.edu, look for Institute for Research in Social Science under Departments and Organizations. For electronic conference discussion of social science data, subscribe to SOS-DATA using steps listed above with e-mail to LISTSERV@UNC.EDU.

- For Psycoloquy Article (with responses) proposing archiving and access on the Internet of data gathered in psychology research, gopher to GOPHER.CIC.NET, choose to look under Electronic Serials, then look under the Alphabetical list, then choose P, and go to Psycoloquy. Next choose 1992.volume.3, and then find items psyc.92.3.29, psyc.92.3.55, psyc.92.3.56, and psyc.92.3.57, the articles by Skoyles, Graham, Gelobter, and Jennings, respectively.

Writing Papers
- For links to labs providing general guidance for writing papers, use http://owl.trc.purdue.edu/writing-labs.html.
- Guidance has also been available for using the APA publication manual. Gopher to gopher.uiuc.edu, and look under Libraries and Reference Information; choose Writer's Workshop Online Handbook. Or, use http://owl.trc.purdue.edu/by-topic.html, and look for APA Format under Research Paper Writing.

People
To locate people, connecting to the place of employment can help. A number of approaches are available. For one, gopher to GOPHER.ND.EDU, look under Non-Notre Dame Information Sources, and then under Phone Books—Other Institutions.

Organizations, Institutes, and Psychology Departments
As already seen above, numerous organizations, institutes, and departments have begun to develop and use Internet to provide services. The following is a sampling of additional sites/offerings which have been available from major organizations in psychology, related organizations, and psychology departments. To locate the address (e.g., gopher or HTTP) of other organizations, phonebooks as noted above under PEOPLE can help; alternatively, single or two-word keyword searches with the search tools mentioned in the opening of this article might be helpful (e.g., http://webcrawler.cs.washington.edu/WebCrawler/WebIndexes.html).
- American Psychological Association. Gopher to GOPHER.APA.ORG, or use http://www.apa.org.
- American Psychological Society. Use http://www.hanover.edu/psych/APS/aps.html.

- American Educational Research Association. Gopher to ASUVM.INRE.ASU. EDU, and look under LISTSERV files.
- The graduate student PsycGRAD project. Gopher to panda1.uottawa.ca and look under PSYCGRAD, or use http://www.cc.utexas.edu/psycgrad/ psycgrad.html.
- For a list of psychology departments on the Internet, use http:// www.hanover.edu/psych/hanpsyc.html, and look under Student Information.
- For a departmental site pertaining to psychiatry, including links to virtual hospital sites, use http://www.med.umich.edu/psychiatry/homepage.html
- Finally, a sample of Cognitive Science/Neuroscience sites:
    - Institute for Research in Cognitive Science. Use http://www.cis. upenn.edu/~ircs/homepage.html
    - The Salk Institute. Use http://salk.edu/
    - The Beckman Institute. Use http://www.beckman.uiuc.edu/
    - Georgia Tech. Use http://www.cc.gatech.edu/cogsci/cogsci.html
    - University of California at Davis. Use http://neuroscience.ucdavis. edu/index.html
    - UCLA. Use http://www.lifesci.ucla.edu/repository/cogsci/

Reprinted from C&RL News, *Vol. 54, No. 9, October 1993. Revised January 1995.*

Internet resources for religious studies

Jeffrey Coon

The Internet provides access to a multitude of resources relevant to religious studies. An invaluable introduction is *The Electric Mystic's Guide to the Internet* by Michael Strangelove (Ottawa, Ontario: M. Strangelove, 1993). It is a nearly comprehensive directory of religion-related online discussion groups, electronic serials, file archives and other resources. The current version is available via FTP from the node PANDA1.UOTTAWA.CA in the directory /pub/religion/ as the files:

electric-mystics-guide-v1.txt
electric-mystics-guide-v3.txt

You can also receive *The Electric Mystic's Guide* via e-mail by sending the following message to LISTSERV@UOTTAWA:

get mystics v1-txt
get mystics v3-txt

Locating online discussion groups

A thorough listing of major online discussion groups in all disciplines is Diane Kovacs' *Directory of Scholarly Electronic Conferences* (Kent, Ohio: Kent State University Libraries). The religious studies section describes over 25 groups. To retrieve it, FTP KSUVXA.KENT.EDU and get the file ACADLIST.FILE4 from the /library/ directory. You may also wish to get the ACADLIST.README file, which contains helpful explanatory notes.

Jeffrey Coon is reference librarian at Indiana University at Kokomo; e-mail: jcoon@ucs.indiana.edu

Alternatively, send the following e-mail message to LISTSERV@KENTVM:
   get acadlist.file4
   get acadlist.readme

Another way to locate groups is to send the command LIST GLOBAL /***
(where *** is a subject keyword such as RELIGION) as an e-mail message to
any valid listserv address. The result will be a list of discussion groups
whose titles or descriptions contain that keyword, sent to you as an e-mail
message.

Selected online discussion groups

Following are a few examples of the wide variety of groups available. Most
can be joined by sending the e-mail message "SUBSCRIBE Groupname
YourName" to LISTSERV@NODE, where NODE is the part of the group
address after the "@" symbol. For example, to subscribe to AIBI-L@UOTTAWA,
Jane Doe would send the e-mail message: "SUBSCRIBE AIBI-L Jane Doe" to
LISTSERV@UOTTAWA. Exceptions to this procedure are noted.

As indicated, some discussion groups also appear as newsgroups on
Usenet, a network available at many universities.

• AIBI-L@UOTTAWA or AIBI-L@ACADVM1.UOTTAWA.CA focuses on the
computerized analysis of Biblical texts.

• AMERCATH@UKCC or AMERCATH@UKCC.UKY.EDU provides a forum
for discussion among scholars and teachers of the history of American Ca-
tholicism.

• ATLANTIS@HARVARDA or ATLANTIS@HARVARDA.HARVARD.EDU (American Theological Library Association Networked Theological Information Service) promotes professional communication among members of ATLA and
other interested persons. To request subscription, contact CWILL@HARVARDA
or CWILL@HARVARDA.HARVARD.EDU.

• BUDDHA-L@ULKYVM or BUDDHA-L@ULKYVM.LOUISVILLE.EDU is an
open forum for exchange of information and views on topics related to
Buddhism and Buddhist studies.

• ELENCHUS@UOTTAWA or ELENCHUS@ACADVM1.UOTTAWA.CA dis-
cusses Christian thought and literature from AD 100 to AD 500. Messages in
English or French are welcome.

• FEMREL-L@MIZZOU1 or FEMREL-MIZZOU1.MISSOURI.EDU encourages
discussion on women and religion and feminist theology.

• IOUDAIOS@YORKVM1 or IOUDAIOS@VM1.YORKU.CA concentrates on
discussion of first-century Judaism and Christian origins, particularly the
works of Philo of Alexandria and Flavius Josephus. Knowledge of Greek is
helpful. ("IOUDAIOS" is Greek for "Jew".)

- ISLAM-L@ULKYVM or ISLAM-L@ULKYVM.LOUISVILLE.EDU carries non-sectarian discussion and debate for scholars and students of the history of Islam.
- JUDAICA@TAUNIVM or JUDAICA@TAUNIVM.TAU.AC.IL invites exchange of information and discussion of work in progress, electronic applications and new approaches which relate to Judaic studies. Participation by a broad audience is encouraged.
- OBJ-REL@EMUVM1 or OBJ-REL@EMUVM1.CC.EMORY.EDU seeks objective discussions of religion and its roles in society.
- RELIGION@HARVARDA or RELIGION@HARVARDA.HARVARD.EDU is sponsored by the Harvard Center for the Study of World Religions. Its purpose is to foster scholarly discussion of the historical or comparative study and teaching of religions. (It is not a forum for personal statements of faith.)
- SSREL-L@UTKVM1 or SSREL-L@UTKVM1.UTK.EDU (Scientific Study of Religion) focuses on the study of religion by scholars in various disciplines.

Usenet newsgroups

Usenet is an international computer network available at many universities. Contact your computer center for further information on access. As noted, some newsgroups also exist as Internet discussion groups. Note: Not all newsgroups are available at all sites. Usenet news groups on religion are: alt.atheism, alt.hindu, clari.news.religion, rec.music.christian, soc.culture.jewish, soc.religion.christian, soc.religion.christian.bible-study, soc.religion.eastern, soc.religion.islam (also RELIGION-ISLAM-REQUEST@NCAR.UCAR.EDU), soc.religion.quaker, talk.origins (creation/evolution discussions), talk.religion.misc, talk.religion.newage.

Electronic journals and newsletters

There are a growing number of journals and newsletters available through the Internet. Typically, they are retrievable through FTP or e-mail, but increasingly they are also available through GOPHER.

- Bryn Mawr Classical Review publishes reviews of current work in Greek and Roman studies. To subscribe, send the e-mail message "SUBSCRIBE BMCR-L" to LISTSERV@CC.BRYNMAWR.EDU.
- A Byte of Torah and A Megabyte of Torah are companion publications. Byte is a weekly newsletter providing analysis of Torah verses; Megabyte is a more detailed monthly publication. To subscribe, send the e-mail message "SUBSCRIBE BYTETORAH" to LISTSERV@ISRAEL.NYSERNET.ORG.
- IOUDAIOS Review is the review journal of IOUDAIOS@YORKVM1, the discussion group on first-century Judaism and Christian origins. It is

distributed to members of IOUDAIOS. (See "Selected online discussion groups" above.)

• Offline is a column by Robert Kraft which has appeared for a number of years in The Bulletin of the Council of Societies for the Study of Religion and in Religious Studies News. It concentrates on the use of computers in religious studies. Distribution is to members of IOUDAIOS.

• Religious Studies Publications Journal—CONTENTS intends to serve as a comprehensive source of information on pedagogical and research resources in religious studies. It electronically archives reviews, abstracts, conference papers, theses and dissertations, bibliographies, and other documents and announces their availability to subscribers. It is not a discussion group. To subscribe, send the e-mail message "SUBSCRIBE CONTENTS YourName" to LISTSERV@UOTTAWA or LISTSERV@ACADVM1.UOTTAWA.CA. To receive full texts of reviews and book notes announced in Religious Studies Publications Journal—CONTENTS, send the message "SUBSCRIBE REVIEW-L YourName" to the same addresses.

Other resources

• CCAT GOPHER: Point your GOPHER at CCAT.SAS.UPENN.EDU (or telnet to that address and login as "gopher"). The University of Pennsylvania Humanities Department and Center for Computer Analysis of Texts (CCAT) provide a collection of humanities course materials and electronic texts through this GOPHER, including sacred texts which can be searched electronically and retrieved, course syllabi, glossaries, essays, and various information files. It also provides a wide variety of Internet-related documents and connections to other humanities-related GOPHERs.

• Johns Hopkins University Press Online Database: Tables of contents and abstracts are available several months in advance for Journal of Early Christian Studies and other journals. To access them, FTP JHUNIX.HCF.JHU.

EDU. Login as "anonymous" and give your Internet address as the password. Get the jcearl-f and jcearl-p files from the /JHU_Press/.zjournals/.class/ directory. These files are also available through the GOPHER at JHUNIX.HCF.JHU.EDU.

• Electronic Buddhist Archives: A world-wide repository of files for researchers of Buddhism, Taoism, and other Asian religions. FTP WUARCHIVE.WUSTL.EDU, login as "anonymous", and explore the directory /doc/coombspapers/otherarchives/electronic-buddhist-archives/.

• JewishNet—The Global Jewish Information Network Project: An electronic clearinghouse for a wide variety of information relevant to Jewish studies. You can connect to online catalogs at Jewish libraries or find out about other file servers, online discussion groups, archives and documents. Telnet to VMS.HUJI.AC.IL and login as "jewishnet".

• Locating sacred texts and related software: Access ARCHIE on a GO-PHER or telnet to ARCHIE and search for PROG ***, where *** is the name of a text, such as Bible or Quran. You will receive a listing of related resources. PROG BIBLE, for example, produces a long listing of Bible text files and study software which can be retrieved via FTP.

• Cruising the FTP sites: FTP PANDA1.UOTTAWA.CA and go to the /pub/ religion/directory. This is the home of the CONTENTS Project archives, including bibliographies, a directory of religious studies scholars, reviews of online discussion groups, theses, dissertations and more. Get the file ftp-index.txt for a helpful overview. FTP ISRAEL.NYSERNET.ORG for a vast archive of material on contemporary Judaism and Israel. Included are the complete text of the Tanach and accompanying commentary, online discussion group archives, Hebrew fonts, and other software.

Reprinted from C&RL News, *Vol. 54, No. 11, December 1993. Revised January 1995.*

Internet sources of government information

Blake Gumprecht

The Internet, the global computer network that is becoming an increasingly valuable source of information on a wide variety of subjects, has proven an especially rich resource for government information, in part because works produced by the U.S. government àre not eligible for copyright protection.

While government agencies have been criticized for not making more information available online, enterprising librarians, professors, business people, and watchdog groups have themselves made a wealth of information available via the network. Internet users can now access hundreds of sources of current government information—census data, Supreme Court decisions, weather forecasts, the *Federal Register,* daily White House press briefings, Bureau of Commerce reports, and much more.

More and more government agencies too are beginning to establish systems that can be accessed remotely. You can now e-mail the President, and passage of the Government Printing Office (GPO) Electronic Information Access Improvement Act of 1993 assures GPO's role in distributing information electronically will increase. A variety of other proposals suggest that in the future, an ever-increasing volume of government information will be available online, sometimes exclusively.

In many cases, there are significant advantages to the sources accessible online over what can be found in the library or via other means. Internet resources are often more up-to-date than their paper counterparts. Frequently

Blake Gumprecht is documents librarian at Temple University Libraries, Philadelphia; e-mail: gumpbw@vm.temple.edu or gumpbw@templevm

they can be searched by keyword. Sometimes they provide information simply not available in more traditional formats. A word of warning is necessary, though. Internet resources are constantly changing. What is available one minute may not be available the next. Source and file names are often changed without notice.

This article presents a sample of Internet sources of government information and was culled from a longer list created for users at Temple University. The sources listed are intended to provide the simplest route to the information described. The preferred source is often a gopher source because of the ease of using the gopher software. Often, however, there are several sources for the same information. When the source listed is a gopher source, the instructions assume users can escape the local gopher menu structure to connect directly to a remote gopher. This can normally be done by issuing the gopher command in combination with a remote system address from your system's ready prompt.

The longer version of the guide can be retrieved electronically from the University of Michigan's Clearinghouse of Subject-Oriented Internet Resource Guides (source: gopher gopher.lib.umich.edu/general reference resources/clearinghouse . . ./guides on the social sciences/government . . .) or the NorthWestNet ftp archive (source: ftp ftp.nwnet.net/user:anonymous/password:ident/cd user-docs/cd government/get gumprecht-guide.txt).

In the list that follows, the "source" is the "address" of the remote computer where the information can be found, along with the "path" a user must take to locate the directory or file that contains the information. Slashes in the source separate commands, steps, or levels in a menu or file hierarchy.

General Resources

• Catalog of Federal Domestic Assistance: Provides information about more than 1,000 U.S. government assistance programs. Searchable by keyword. *Source:* gopher marvel.loc.gov/federal government information/federal information resources/information by agency/general information resources.

• Copyright Information: Library of Congress system allows users to search information about works registered in the U.S. Copyright Office since 1978. *Source:* telnet locis.loc.gov.

• Federal Information Exchange: Provides information about federal education and research programs, scholarships, fellowships, grants, programs for minorities, procurement opportunities, and more. *Source:* gopher fedix.fie.com.

• Federal Jobs: Lists thousands of U.S. government job openings taken from a variety of federal computer bulletin boards. *Source:* gopher dartcms1.dartmouth.edu/job openings in the federal government.

• FedWorld: National Technical Information Service system provides access to more than 100 U.S. government computer bulletin boards. Also includes full text of select government publications, statistical files, federal job lists, and more. *Source:* telnet fedworld.gov.
• Geographic Names Database: Provides latitude and longitude, county and state location, elevation, and more for thousands of places in the U.S. Searchable by place name or zip code. *Source:* gopher gopher.micro. umn.edu/libraries/reference works/u.s. geographic names database.
• Library of Congress Information System: Provides access to the library's online catalog, copyright files, databases containing information on federal legislation and foreign law, and more. *Source:* telnet locis.loc.gov.
• Library of Congress Marvel: One-stop source for a multitude of government material—Congressional information, census data, White House documents, State Department reports, and more. *Source:* gopher marvel.loc.gov.
• National Weather Service Forecasts: Provides forecasts, current conditions, information on earthquakes, and more for the 50 states and Canada. *Source:* gopher ashpool.micro.umn.edu/weather.
• State Department Travel Advisories: An archive of State Department travel information and advisories arranged by country. Files include country descriptions, current conditions, entry requirements, embassy locations, information about medical facilities, drug penalties and more. *Source:* gopher gopher.stolaf.edu/internet resources.
• *World Factbook* (1990–1992): Full text of the CIA-produced annual which provides information about the geography, people, government, and economy of countries around the world. *Source:* gopher wiretap.spies.com/ electronic books/cia world factbook.

Political science, law, and government
• Budget of the United States Government: Full text of the proposed budget for the 1994 fiscal year; can be searched by keyword. *Source:* gopher sunsite.unc.edu/worlds of sunsite/us and world politics/proposed budget.
• Campaign '92 and Election Results: Full text of key position papers, speeches, press releases, and more from major candidates in the 1992 presidential election. *Source:* gopher tamuts.tamu.edu/browse information by subject/political science.
• Code of Federal Regulations: Commercial system allows users to browse the code or search it by keyword. Access to the complete CFR is not yet available. System places limits on the amount of information nonsubscribers can retrieve. *Source:* gopher gopher.netsys.com/counterpoint publishing.
• Congressional Directories: Library of Congress system provides access to a variety of directories. *Source:* gopher marvel.loc.gov/u.s. congress.

- Congressional Information: Provides access to directories, committee rosters, NAFTA documents, the Americans with Disabilities Act, and more. *Source:* gopher gopher.lib.umich.edu/social sciences resources/government and politics/u.s. government resources: legislative branch.
- Congressional Legislation: Library of Congress system allows users to search files that describe and track legislation introduced in Congress from 1973 to present. *Source:* telnet locis.loc.gov/federal legislation.
- Executive Branch Resources: Provides access to executive branch directories, White House information, NAFTA documents, and more. *Source:* gopher gopher.lib.umich.edu/social sciences resources/government and politics/u.s. government resources: executive branch.
- *Federal Register:* Commercially produced system allows users to browse or search the daily *Federal Register.* System places limits on the amount of information nonsubscribers can retrieve. *Source:* gopher gopher.netsys.com/ counterpoint publishing.
- National Performance Review: Full text of the report of Vice-President Al Gore's task force on reinventing government. *Source:* gopher sunsite.unc. edu/worlds of sunsite/us and world politics.
- Presidential Documents from the *Federal Register:* Full text of presidential proclamations, executive orders, and other documents. *Source:* gopher gopher.netsys.com/counterpoint publishing/federal register/selected agencies.
- Supreme Court Decisions: Full text of decisions issued since 1989. *Source:* gopher info.umd.edu/educational resources/united states.
- Treaties and International Covenants: Full text of major treaties. *Source:* gopher fatty.law.cornell.edu/foreign and international law/multilateral treaties.
- United Nations: Full text of U.N. press releases, U.N. Conference on Environment and Development reports, United Nations Development Programme documents, telephone directories, and more. *Source:* gopher nywork1.undp.org.
- White House Information: Full text of policy statements, press briefings, speeches, the president's daily schedule, and more. *Source:* gopher tamuts.tamu.edu/browse information by subject/political science/information from the white house. *Source:* gopher sunsite.unc.edu/worlds of sunsite/ us and world politics/sunsite political science archives/whitehouse-papers.
- World Constitutions: Full text of constitutions of countries worldwide. *Source:* gopher wiretap.spies.com/government docs. Other constitutions can be accessed by conducting a gopher Veronica search, using "constitution" as the keyword.

Social sciences and humanities
• AskERIC: Archive of education information compiled by an Internet question-answering service for educators at Syracuse University. *Source:* gopher ericir.syr.edu.
• Bureau of Justice Statistics Documents: Full text of select Bureau publications. *Source:* gopher uacsc2.albany.edu/united nations justice network.
• Census of Population and Housing: 1990 Census data available for U.S. cities, counties, metropolitan areas, states, and the nation, with comparisons from 1980. *Source:* gopher bigcat.missouri.edu/reference center.
• Criminal Justice Country Profiles: Full text of a series of U.N. reports on crime and criminal justice in 123 countries. *Source:* gopher uacsc2.albany.edu/united nations justice network/u.n. criminal justice country profiles.
• Economic Bulletin Board: Department of Commerce system provides access to thousands of files containing information about current economic conditions, economic indicators, employment, trade, and more in 20 general subject areas. *Source:* gopher gopher.lib.umich.edu/social sciences research/economics. *Source:* telnet ebb.stat-usa.gov.
• Educational Resources Information Center (ERIC): Provides keyword access to abstracts of articles and publications about education. *Source:* gopher spc.syr.edu/local resources.
• Gross State Product Tables: Provides access to U.S. Bureau of Economic Analysis tables estimating the value of goods and services for 61 industries in 50 states. *Source:* gopher gopher.lib.umich.edu/social sciences research/economics.
• North American Free Trade Agreement: Full text of NAFTA and related documents. *Source:* gopher cyfer.esusda.gov/americans communicating electronically.
• Radio Free Europe/Radio Liberty Research Institute Daily Report: Full text of a daily digest of developments in Russia, Transcaucasia and Central Asia, Central and Eastern Europe. *Source:* gopher gopher.lib.umich.edu/news services.
• Statistics Canada Daily Reports: Full text of daily statistical releases, lists of publications, and more from Canada's primary compiler of statistics. *Source:* telnet info.carleton.ca/terminal type:decvt100. Physical sciences, health, and medicine
• AIDS Information: Provides AIDS statistics, daily summaries of newspaper articles about AIDS, full text of *AIDS Treatment News,* reports from the National Commission on AIDS, and more. *Source:* gopher gopher.niaid.nih.gov.
• CancerNet: Full text of National Cancer Institute fact sheets, publications, patient diagnosis statements, and more. *Source:* gopher helix.nih.gov/health and clinical information.

• Chemical Substance Fact Sheets: Full text of EPA fact sheet about hundreds of chemicals. Can be browsed or searched by keyword. *Source:* gopher ecosys.drdr.virginia.edu/education/environmental fact sheets.

• Cooperative Extension System: Department of Agriculture system provides access to extension service reports, directories, nutritional data, and more. *Source:* gopher esusda.gov.

• Earthquake Information: Provides data about recent earthquakes worldwide. *Source:* gopher gopher.stolaf.edu/internet resources/weather and geography.

• Food and Drug Administration Bulletin Board System: Full text of FDA news releases, enforcement reports, import alerts, drug and product approval lists, *Federal Register* summaries, articles from *FDA Consumer,* and more. *Source:* telnet fdabbs.fda.gov/login:bbs.

• Health Security Act: Full text of the Clinton administration's health plan and related documents. Act can be browsed or searched by keyword. *Source:* gopher sunsite.unc.edu/worlds of sunsite/us and world politics/national health security plan.

• *Morbidity and Mortality Weekly Report:* Full text of the Centers for Disease Control and Prevention weekly publication. *Source:* gopher gopher.niaid.nih.gov/aids related information.

• National Institutes of Health: Provides access to NIH phone books, calendars, library catalogs, molecular biology databases, *NIH Guide for Grants and Contracts,* and more. *Source:* gopher gopher.nih.gov.

• National Science Foundation: Provides access to grant information, NSF directories, press releases, full text of foundation publications, and more. *Source:* gopher stis.nsf.gov.

• PENpages: Pennsylvania State University system provides the full text of thousands of documents about agriculture, food and nutrition, family issues, and more. *Source:* telnet psupen.psu.edu/username:penpages.

• Spacelink: NASA system provides access to shuttle status reports, mission summaries, NASA news releases, and other files with current and historical information about NASA. *Source:* telnet spacelink.msfc.nasa.gov/username:newuser/password:newuser.

• World Health Organization: Provides access to world health statistics, full text of selected WHO publications, and more. *Source:* gopher gopher.who.ch.

Reprinted from C&RL News, *Vol. 55, No. 1, January 1994.*

African studies computer resources

Patricia S. Kuntz

This paper focuses on African studies computer resources readily available in the North America with linkages to Africa. Africanists can utilize four fundamental computer systems: Internet/Bitnet, Fidonet, Usenet, and dial-up bulletin board system (BBS). Comprehensive lists of these network services are available from Arthur McGee.[1]

Internet/Bitnet
The most common network systems throughout the world are Internet and the various compatible networks, and to a lesser degree, Bitnet.
• INTERNET. Nearly all U.S. and Canadian universities subscribe to the Internet. Users of the Internet can access distribution lists, Telnet, File Transfer Protocol (FTP), Gophers, and World Wide Web as described below. Most Internet sites also have access to Usenet newsgroups.
• BITNET. Bitnet's main feature is the automatic mailing program called Listserv. Although most universities have eliminated their Bitnet services in favor of Internet, Africanists can connect with Listservs through gateways from the Internet.
A. Electronic Mail
   Both networks provide electronic mail (E-mail) for sending public and private messages. Contacts to Africanists and African scholars or inquiries concerning African studies can be made through the following organizations

Patricia S. Kuntz is outreach director of the African Studies Program at the University of Wisconsin-Madison; bitnet: kuntz@wiscmacc; Internet: kuntz@macc.wisc.edu

and federally funded Title VI National Resource Centers for African Studies (ASC) in Table 1. (see Appendix A for complete description of services)

Table 1
African-Related Organizations and African Studies Centers

INSTITUTION	E-MAIL ADDRESS
African Studies Association (ASA)	<africa@emoryu1.cc.emory.edu>
American Association for the Advancement of Science/African Academy of Science (AAAS)	<africa@aaas.org>
Association of African Studies Programs (AASP)	<johns@acpub.duke.edu>
Arab Word and Islamic Resources	<awair@igc.apc.org>
Washington Office on Africa	<woa@igc.apc.org>
* HEA Title VI African Studies Centers *	
Boston University	NA
Bryn Mawr College	<mosirim@cc.brynmawr.edu>
California-Berkeley, University of	<asc@uclink.berkeley.edu>
California-Los Angeles, University of	<keller@polsci.sscnet.ucla.edu>
Central States University (Ohio)	NA
Columbia University	NA
Florida, University of	<africa@africa.ufl.edu>
Haverford College	<hgglickma@haverford.edu>
Howard University	<rjc@scs.howard.edu>
Illinois, University of	<bassett@ux1.cso.uiuc.edu>
Indiana University	<winchest@indiana.edu>
Kansas, University of	<afs@kuhub.cc.ukans.edu>
Lincoln University	<roposek@aol.com>
Michigan State University	<africa@ibm.cis.msu.edu>
Ohio State University	<mowoe.2@osu.edu>
Ohio University	NA
Pennsylvania, University of	<africa@mail.sas.upenn.edu>
Stanford University	<richard.roberts@forsythe.stanford.edu>
Swarthmore College	<rhopkin1@cc.swarthmore.edu>
Tuskegee University	NA
Wisconsin, University of	<afrst@macc.wisc.edu>
Yale University	NA

The African Studies Association now sponsors the Electronic Information Group to promote computer networking among ASA members.[2]

Commercial companies can also provide Internet connections, in addition to a wide variety of other services such as on-line news, weather reports, and so forth. The largest commercial company is CompuServe which provides CompuServe Africa for the growing African demand for network connections especially from southern Africa.[3] Another commercial service for African news is NewsNet.[4] This company has the following products among others:

AFRICA NEWS	ANGOLA PEACE MONITOR
ASP DIPLOMAT	MIDEAST MARKETS
SOUTH AFRICAN FOCUS	SOUTHSCAN--SOUTHERN AFRICA

B. Distribution Lists

Another Internet feature is the option of creating distribution lists. These lists consist of frequently used addresses which form an identifiable interest group. Three levels of control exist for maintaining the service.

Private List. One type of distribution list can be developed and maintained as a privately created list. The list owner has full control and moderates the messages. For this reason, the private list is a one-way service to the subscribers. Michigan State University's ASC distributes their bi-weekly newsletter electronically to subscribers <21248yf@ibm.cis.msu.edu>. The National Foreign Language Center[5] has a private list for officers who represent organizations of the less commonly taught languages including those from the African Language Teachers Association and the American Association of Teachers of Arabic.

Public List. Another type of distribution list is one available to the public. Although a list owner still manages the list, anyone can send messages to it since the list is unmoderated. In order to receive all the messages, a users of this public list must request a subscription from the list owner. Their replies, unless specified to another user, are distributed to all the members.

Table 2 contains a sample of public distribution lists that specialize in African-related discussions.

Table 2
Public Distibution Lists

LIST	FOCUS
aajn@catcc.bitnet	Burkina Faso
afriqnews@athena.mit.edu	African news service
algeria-net-request@monte.svec.uh.edu	Algeria
amazight-net@engcd.bu.edu	Berber
ASA-NET@sfu.ca	African Students' Association
CAMEROON- | unpublished	Cameroonian Students Union in UK
egypt-net-request@das.harvard.edu	Egypt
ETHIOPIA | tesh@cleo.eng.sun.com	Ethiopia
ethiolist-request@netcom.com	Ethiopia
eritrea-net-request@eritrea.ci.net	Eritrea
euro-naija-request@lists.funet.fi	Nigerians in Europe
geez-cev@eritrea.ci.net	Eritrea
islam-news@iastate.edu	News about Islam in English
imnet@max.uwashington.edu	Islamic Word News
kenya-net-request@ftp.com	(for Kenyans only)
kenyanews-request@media.mit.edu	Newspapers from Kenya
kci-net-request@sml1.ecs.umass.edu	Kenyan/East African Tech
maghreb-group@bailey.pcpac.washington.edu	North Africa
mauritanie-net-request@bat710.univ-lyon1.fr	Mauritania
mes@athena.mit.edu	Middle East Students
middle-eastern-music-request@nic.funet.fi	Middle Eastern Music

msa-request@eleceng.ee.queensu.ca	Muslim Student Assn.
msanews-request@magnus.acs.ohio-state.edu	Muslim Student Assn. News
muslimbaynet-request@ocf.berkeley.edu	Muslims in the San Francisco Bay Ares
naijanet@athena.mit.edu	(for Nigerians only)
naija-news-request@welby.med.harvard.edu	Nigerian news
okyeame-request@athena.mit.edu	(for Ghanaians only)
reader@tasha.poly.edu	Computerized Arabic script
saf@athena.mit.edu	African students
sierranet@athena.mit.edu	Sierra Leone discussion
usasa-l@afrex.mcws.fidonet.org	US-South African
ZIMNET ǀ dsaburi@athena.mit.edu	(For Zimbabweans only)

Neither of the above mentioned distribution lists provides any automated features such as archived messages or subscriber addresses, nor do they require a minimum number of subscribers. Rather, a systems operator must retain messages manually and update the address list of subscribers.

Automated List. The Listserv/er and Mailserv software are services that some universities provide for automating the distribution lists. This service customarily requires a minimum of 100 users before a computer center will accept responsibility for posting new users, archiving messages, and maintaining the list. In contrast to the above two distribution lists, users subscribe directly to the software that controls the list's functions. Unfortunately, each software has slightly different procedures for users to manage their own subscription. When a problem occurs, the list owner must intervene.

For instance, the University of Wisconsin provides a forum for readers of Swahili with *Swahili-L* and of Eritrean interests with *Eritrea-L*. Table 3 provides some examples of automated distribution lists.

Table 3
Automated Lists

LIST	SUBSCRIPTION ADDRESS	FOCUS
AFRICA-EIS	listserv@tome.worldbank.org	African Environmental Studies
AFRICA-L	listserv@vtvm1.cc.vt.edu	African-related news
AFRICA-N	listserv@epas.utoronto.ca	African News & Information
AFRICANA	listserv@birds.wm.edu	Info Technology and Africa
ALGNEWS	listserv@gwuvm.gwu.edu	Algeria News List (French)
ARABIC-L	mailserv@byu.edu	American Assn. of Teachers of Arabic
CAMNET	listserv@icinucevm.cnuce.cnr.it	Cameroon Technology
ERITREA-L	listserver@relay.adp.wisc.edu	News of Eritrea
ISLAM-L	listserv@ulkyvm.bitnet	History of Islam
ITISALAT	listserv@guvm.bitnet	Computer Tech. for Arabic
MEH2O-L	listserv@taunivm.tau.ac.il	Middle East Water
MELANET	listserv@cornell.edu	Middle East Librarians
MIAST	listserv@uiucvmd.bitnet	Maghrebian Scientific Institute
MSA-L	listserv@psuvm.psu.edu	Muslim Student Association
MUSLIMS	listserv@asuvm.inre.asu.edu	Islamic Information & News

RINAF-L	listserv@icinucevm.cnuce.cnr.it	Reg. Informatics Net for Africa
SA-DROUGH	listserv@devcan.ca	Southern Africa (Region) Drought
SWAHILI-L	listserver@relay.adp.wisc.edu	Message in Swahili only
TSSACT-L	listserv@utkvm1.bitnet	Tunisian Scientific Society Activities
TSSNEWS	listserv@athena.mit.edu	Tunisian Scientific Society News
TUNINFO	listserv@psuvm.psu.edu	Tunisian Info Office, Washington D.C.
TUNISNET	listserv@psuvm.psu.edu	The Tunisia Network
ZAIRE-L	listserv@ilstu.edu	News of Zaire

C. Telnet

Telnet is a service that allows remote access to computers. In addition to library resources available from this service, Telnet enables the Cleveland Freenet to operate an on-line Islamic school. Below is a sample of African-related Telnet addresses:

crlcataog.uchicago.edu	Cooperative Africana Microform Project
info2.sabinet.co.za	South African Bibliographic and Information Network
freenet-in-a.cwru.edu	Islamic School

D. File Transfer Protocol

The Anonymous File Transfer Protocol (FTP) provides free access for file upload and download. It is not an interactive system but rather a storage system for software, graphics, sounds, and documents. African studies file sites are listed at several directory nodes around the world. To locate FTP sites, Africanists may search "Archie" by specific file names at one of several sites by "telneting."

```
<quiche.cs.mcgill.ca>
<archie.unl.edu>
<archie.rutgers.edu>
      login: archie
      archie>    prog Africa        or
                 prog Mandela       or
                 prog Swahili
```

Regretably, "Archie" does not provide subject searches. Consequently, Africanists will need to be creative in selecting file names. Unfortunately, few ASC universities provide FTP site storage. Some FTP sites are listed in Table 4.

Table 4
FTP Sites

ADDRESS	FOCUS
ftp.loc.gov	The Library of Congress
ftp.cs.columbia.edu/archives/mirror2/faq	soc.culture.arabic
ftp.mcs.kent.edu/pub/islam	Qur'an
ftp.umich.edu/foreign_lang/arabic	Qur'an
ftp.cs.ubc.ca/pub/local/FAQ/african/gen/saoep.txt	Sao Tome & Principe
ftp.spies.com/Library/Religion/Bible/Swahili	New Testament in Swahili
ftp.uu.net/doc/poitics/umich-poli/SNU	Somalia News Update

E. Gopher

The University of Minnesota developed the "Gopher" software to enable information to be more accessible. This technology uses a text file format with menu selections. The Gopher allows users to receive information but not to send. For instance, an Africanist could look up E-mail addresses, course lists, weekly announcements, and faculty departments or search a library catalog systems at universities and organizations around the world. To assist in searches, Africanists can use any of several "Veronica" sites listed on each Gopher server.

Several ASCs contribute information to one of several campus Gophers. The University of Pennsylvania and the University of Wisconsin have created an African Studies client via Gopher.

Table 5
Gopher Clients

CLIENT	FOCUS
wolfnet.com	Africa
gopher.adp.wisc.edu/courses&programs/	African Studies
gopher.cic.net	African Studies On-line
cd.sunysb.edu/pub/EN/_incoming/AbdelHadi_Bukres	Arabic Alphabet
sunny.stat-usa.gov/00/NTDB/Bnotes	Country Notes

F. World Wide Web

At present World Wide Web (WWW) is the most sophisticated interactive technology for browsing resources on the Internet. Since 1992, WWW "homepages" have multiplied from 50 to over 250,000. It is a multi-media hypertext system that enables Africanists to read text, listen to sound, and see moving graphics. In contrast to Gopher, WWW is interactive, allowing for sending and receiving information. This technology also permits Africanists using WWW to link directly to FTP and Gopher for additional information. Like FTP and Gopher, WWW has searching capabilities. The WWW searching softwares "Lycos," "WWW Worm," "WebCrawler," "JumpStation," and "CERN" specialize for user convenience such as searches by page, subject, title, keyword, index, or directory. For example, the "WebCrawler" found 414 documents from the query "Africa." Table 6 provides some WWWs that contain African information.

Table 6
WWW Homepage

HOMEPAGE	FOCUS
http://www.sas.upenn.edu/African_Studies/AS.html	Africa
http://philae.sas.upenn.edu/Arabic/arabic.html	Arabic Lessons
http://www.cc.emory.edu/CARLOS/egypt.gal.html"	Egypt

http://ux1.cso.uiuc.edu/~kagan/cas.html	Center for African Studies
http://www.cs.indiana.edu/hyplan/dmulholl/ab_base.html	Abysinia
http://www.memphis.edu/egypt/egypt.html	Color Tour of Egypt
http://www.mit.edu:8001/activities/Arab/homepage.html	Arabs
http://www.tcom.ohiou.edu/OU_Language/OU_Language.html	Language Courses
http://lcweb.loc.gov/homepage/lchp.html	Library of Congress
http://wiretap.spies.com/0/Gov/Word/malawi.con	Malawi Constitution
http://www.intac.com/PubService/rwanda	Rwanda
http://rubens.anu.edu.au/islam2/index_1.html	Architecture of Islam
http://www.cs.ubc.ca/spider/shaze/africa/africa.html	Africa
http://www.cuug.ab.ca:8001/gubrub/Eritrea.html	Eritrea
http://www.newton.cam.ac.uk/egypt/	Egyptology

The University of Pennsylvania has led the ASCs in outreach services via WWW.[6] Nevertheless, faculty, staff, and students at other ASCs have also created a homepage in an effort to disseminate information about Africa more efficiently: the University of Illinois, Ohio University, Stanford University, and the University of Wisconsin among others.

Fidonet

Fidonet is an international, decentralized, cooperative, voluntary system in which participants serve one another by relaying messages through a routing system. A list of all Fidonet bulletin board systems (BBSs) (known as the "nodelist") is updated weekly from a central point (node 1:1/0) and is distributed throughout the network. Since this network has no central computers, Fidonet is organized in a branching system with six geographically designated zones:

> 1 = USA/Canada/Mexico - North America
> 2 = Europe
> 3 = Australia, New Zealand (Oceana)
> 4 = Latin America
> 5 = Africa
> 6 = Asia

Fidonet nodes may be established by individuals using personal computers, high-speed modems (28,800 baud), and free software. The only overhead costs are telephone charges. Consequently, this process permits access to developing areas by users of the international hosts. For this reason, Fidonet technology is very popular in many African countries and in rural school districts of North America.

Echomail is a specific public forum i.e., conference group or newsgroup. Currently, there are four Echomail conferences of interest to Africanists:

Africa Link	Peace Corps,
South Africa	Southern Africa Drought

Unfortunately, none of the ASCs provide Fidonet points/nodes either for research or outreach purposes.

Usenet News

Usenet is a third worldwide network that provides one mainservice -- news or "gossip." Usenet newsgroups are available to Internet sites and free to the public. Therefore, Usenet newsgroups do not require subscriptions. Messages sent to any of over 5000 newsgroups are stored only for five days and then automatically deleted. No files are associated with this network. Unlike the Internet listserv/ers, Usenet does not provide archiving or digest capabilities. Consequently, few newsgroups are moderated. However, this network provides an important service for "message junkies" who enjoy reading many messages from a variety of newsgroups daily. Not all sites carry Usenet News and those which do, often do not carry all the newsgroups. There are no searching capabilities as with FTP, Gopher, or WWW. Some African-related Usenet News message areas are listed below by discussion focus.

alt.culture.somalia	alt.religion.islam
bit.tech.africana	clari.world.africa
soc.culture.african	soc.culture.arabic
soc.culture.berber	soc.culture.egyptian
soc.culture.maghreb	soc.culture.nigeria
soc.culture.somalia	soc.culture.southafrica
soc.religion.islam	rec.music.afro-latin
rec.travel	talk.politics.mideast

Bulletin Board System

The bulletin board system (BBS) connects personal computers directly through a telephone connection. Since these boards cost the user a telephone call, unlike the academic network (Internet), a long distance log-in can be expensive.

Presently, few BBSs exist for strictly African-related content. Only one African Studies Association member now operates a BBS.

Baobab (1989) Bob Barad (202) 296-9790 8 N 1 1200/2400/9600/14,400 modem
Fidonet connection   1:109/151
Internet connections   @f151.n109.z1.fidonet.org or bob@baobab.com

This particular BBS provides Internet and Fidonet connectivity that enables subscriber to send and receive messages to several BBSs or node sites in African countries.

African Linkages

For Africanists seeking direct contacts in Africa, over 30 African countries offer network connections. Larry Landweber (founding member of the In-

ternet Society) at Wisconsin provides a bi-annual update of the five network options for each African country. This information is available through
the Internet Society electronically:

E-mail	<isoc@isoc.org>
FTP	<FTP.cs.wisc.edu /connectivity_table/version_12.text>
Gopher	<gopher.isoc.org>
WWW	http://info.isoc.org/home.html

Table 7
Connectivity in Africa by Country, Code, and Network

Angola DZ: IU		
Botswana BW: FU	Burkina Faso BF: U	
Cameroon CM: U	Congo CG: U	Cote d'Ivoire CI: U
Egypt EG: BIU	Eritrea ER: F	Ethiopia ET: F
Gambia GM: F	Ghana GH: F	Guinea GN: U
Kenya KE: F		
Lesotho LS: U		
Madagascar MG: FU	Mali ML: U	Mauritius MU: F
	Morocco MA: U	Mozambique MZ:U
Namibia NA: FU	Niger NE: U	Nigeria NG: F
Reunion RE: U		
Senegal SN: FU	Seychelles SC: U	South Africa ZA: FIU
	Swaziland SW: F	
Tanzania TZ: F	Togo TG: U	Tunisia TN: BFIU
Uganda UG: F		
Zambia ZM: FIU	Zimbabwe ZW: FU	

B=Bitnet, F=Fidonet, I=Internet, U=UUCP

For Francophone countries having UUCP service (Table 4), contact the
director of ORSTOM Paul Renaud <renaud@ostom.fr>. Mike Lawrie
<mlawrie@apies.frd.ac.za> of Uninet Foundation for Research Development can
provide information concerning connectivity among the countries of Southern Africa. To complement Landweber's list, Randy Bush has assembled
Connectivity with Africa, a directory of specific addresses and networks in
Africa. It is available by Gopher or WWW:

Gopher:	<server@gopher.psg.com>
	pub/gopher-data/networks/connect/africa.txt
WWW:	gopher://gopher.psg.com:70/0/0/networks/connect/africa.txt

A. E-Mail

Private, non-governmental organizations provide E-mail connectivity for
many countries whose government does not presently have the resources
to maintain electronic services. These organizations, having North American, European, or United Nations sponsor, provide E-mail and other net-

work services for their (Table 7) staff's services.[7] The actual technology varies among Internet, Bitnet, Fidonet, and UUCP.

Table 8
Private, Non-Governmental Organization Networks

NETWORK		COUNTRY - SYSOP
ARCCNET	(African Regional Center for Computing)	Kenya: S. Ochuodho
CABECA	(Capacity Building for Electronic Communication in Africa)	
CGNET	(Consulting Group on International Agricultural Research)	
ELCI	(Environment Liaison Centre International)	Kenya: D. Rigby
ENDA-TM	(Environment and Development in the Third World)	Senegal: M. Fall
GHASTINET	(Council for Scientific and Industrial Research)	Ghana: A. Mahamadu
HEALTHNET		
MANGO	(Micro Access for Non-Governmental Organizations)	Zimbabwe: R. Stringer
PADISNET	(Pan African Development Information System-UNECA)	Ethiopia: L. Adam
RINAF	(Regional Informatics Network for Africa-UNESCO)	multiple
RIONET	(Riseau Inter-tropical d'Ordinaateurs-ORSTOM)	multiple

B. FTP

A few Anonymous FTP sites are available in Egypt and South Africa such as those listed below:

> Egypt
>> ftp.auc-sas.eun.eg
>
> South Africa:

ftp.ru.ac.za	Rhodes University
ftp.wn.apc.org	African National Congress
ftp.wmai.misanet.org	Media Institute of Southern Africa

C. Gopher

Gopher technology managed by individuals or organizations in three countries is providing information for international use.

> Egypt:
>> American University in Cairo/
>
> South Africa:
>> African National Congress Information/
>> J.S.Gericke Library, University of Stellenbosch/
>> Rhodes University Computing Centre, Grahamstown, South Africa/
>> South African Bibliographic and Information Network/
>> The Foundation for Research Development/
>> The Internetworking Company of Southern Africa (TICSA)/
>> University of Natal (Durban)/
>> University of Natal, Durban (ZA) - Elec.Eng./
>> University of Pretoria/

> University of Pretoria, South Africa/
> University of South Africa (Unisa), Pretoria/
> University of Stellenbosch/
> University of the Witwatersrand, South Africa - Computer Science D../

Tunisia:

> The Tunisian Gopher server/

D. *World Wide Web*

Although WWW service requires powerful computers and money for support, several countries offer this service. Most of the African WWWs are academic; however, ten other WWWs provide information on tourism, investments, and computing. Some of the more common WWWs are listed below:

Egypt:

> http://auc-amer.eun.eg

South Africa:

> http://www.ru.ac.za Rhodes University Computing Services
> http://www.cs.wit.ac.za/faq/africa/africa.html
> http://www.is.co.za/wmail.html

E. *News Groups*

The equivalent service to Usenet News in South Africa is the "ZA." The *"Networking in Southern Africa"* file at the Rhodes University Gopher listed below explains the service. Messages can be sent by changing all the "." to "-" in the list below and then add "quagg.ru.ac.za" as indicated.

> <za-xx@quagg.ru.ac.za>
>
> za.culture.xhosa   za.environment   za.politics   za.schools

F. *Bulletin Board System*

South Africa has a wide variety and over 100 bulletin boards.[8] Most North Americans would not use these BBSs because of the prohibitive cost of the long distance telephone call resulting from the connection.

Within the past year, a variety of computer networks in African countries have linked North American scholars with their counterparts. Moreover, these networks have allowed researchers, business persons, government officials to work efficiently. Combinations of these networks have enabled even middle school students in Milwaukee, Wisconsin (U.S.) to communicate with like students in Mamelodi, Transvaal (S.A.).[9]

Conclusion

The four computer networks briefly described above and the variety of services which they provide are fundamental tools for Africanists. With the increased demand for computer networking, technicians are developing interactive software that allow users to access simultaneously these four networks. As such, these networks should be readily available and be used by administrators, faculty, students, librarians, and outreach personnel in connecting with others interested in Africa. Proficiency in computer technology, including the manipulation of these computer networks, has become an essential for Africanists in research, teaching, administration, and extension.

Notes

1. For a complete list of files, contact Arthur McGee at:
   Internet: <amcgee@netcom.com> <amcgee@eis.ca.state.edu>
   Compuserve: [72377,1351] Voice: [1-31--320-BYTE]
   AFRIMAIL.MSG=Internet Mailing Lists
   AFRISITE.MSG=Online Information Sites
   AFRINEWS.MSG=Usenet Newsgroups
   BLACKBBS.MSG=BBS List
2. Richard Chowning (Abeline Christian University) has let this group for over three years. He maintains an FTP site for papers on computer networking from the ASA meetings <chowning@acuvax.acu.edu>.

Fung, K. (1994). Africa on the internet selected resources. Stanford, CA: Hoover Institution (manuscript prepared for the African Studies Association-Electronic Information Group.

Cajee, M. (1994). The guide to Islamic resources on the internet. [available from ftp.netcom.com/pub/mcgee/african/islam/cybermuslim.guide]

Roberts, J.W. (1994). Middle East/North Africa internet resource guide. Salt Lake City, UT; University of Utah, Middle East Studies Cneter (manuscript). [available on gopher-University of Utah and at <sunsite.unc.edu>]
3. News release 3 September 1992. In the United States contact Compuserve directly. In South Africa (012) 841-2530 or Southern Africa (+27)(12) 841-2530.
4. NewsNet: For the Business Information Edge. Contact: Kelly Bahel, Newsnet, Account Rep, 945 Haverford Road, Bryn Mawr, PA 19010 (215) 527-8030, (800) 952-0122.
5. Contact: Betsy Hart, NFLC, % Johns Hopkins University, 1619 Massachusetts Ave., NW, Washington, DC 20036.
6. Sysop is Ali Ali-Dinar, Outreach Director <aadinar@mail.sas.upenn.edu>
7. Shoneboom, J. (1992). *Electronic networking in Africa: Advancing science and technology for development,* Washington, DC: American Association of the Advancement of Science–African Program.

Lewis, S.G. & Samoff, J. (1992). *Microcomputers in African development: Critical perspectives.* Boulder, CO: Westview Press.

White, W.D. (1994). Technology fact sheets: Information and communication technologies for Africa. Washington, DC: National Research Council, Board on Science and Technology for International Development.

8. Fisher, R. (1993). BBS list South Africa. [forwarded document from the University of Potchefstroom, South Africa, on <alt.bbe.lists>]

9. Contact: John Thompson (Fritsche Middle School) <thompson@omnifest. uwn.edu> or Patrick Beddy (SOS Children's Village) <patrick@sos.pta. school.za> For a complete list of secondary schools in South Africa with internet connections check the newsgroup for South Africa <za.schools>.

Reprinted from C&RL News, *Vol. 55, No. 2, February 1994. Revised January 1995.*

Appendix A

Networking Capabilities Organizations and African Studies Centers
USED Funding AY 1994-97[1]

	E-Mail Addresses Center/Contact/Director	Bib	LC	OD	Distribution List/listserv	FTP	Gopher	WWW	Fidonet	BBS
AAAS	african@aaas.org	-	-	-	-	-	-	-	-	-
AASP	johns@acpub.due.edu	-	-	-	-	-	-	-	-	-
ALA	ava@cornela.cit.cornell.edu	-	-	-	-	-	-	-	-	-
ALTA	folarin@macc.wisc.edu	-	Yes	Yes	Swahili-L	-	-	-	-	-
ASA	africa@emoryu1.cc.emory.edu	-	-	-	-	-	-	-	-	-
WOA	woa@igc.apc.org	-	-	-	-	-	-	-	-	-
BU	No	Yes	Yes	Yes	amazigh-net	-	No	No	-	-
UCB	asc@uclink.berkeley.edu	Yes	Yes	-	muslimbaynet	-	Yes	No	-	-
UCLA	keller@polsci.sscnet.ucla.edu	?	Yes	Yes		-	No	No	-	-
CSU	No		No	-		-	-	-	-	-
CU	?	Yes	No	-		Yes	-	-	-	-
FL	africa@africa.ufl.edu	Yes	Yes	Yes		-	Yes	-	-	-
HU	?	?	No	No		-	No	-	-	-
IL	bassett@ux1.cso.uiuc.edu	Yes	Yes	Yes		Yes	Yes	Yes	-	-
IN	winchest@indiana.edu	Yes	Yes	Yes		-	No	Yes	-	-
KS	afs@kuhub.cc.ukans.edu	Yes	Yes	-	KU-African	No	No	No	-	-
LU	roposek@aol.com	-	-	-		-	-	-	-	-
MSU	africa@ibm.cis.msu.edu	Yes	Yes	Yes	newsletter	No	Yes	No	-	-
OSU	mowoe.2@osu.edu	-	No	-	msanews	-	Yes	No	-	-
OU	No	-	?	-		-	Yes	Yes	-	-
PA	africa@mail.sas.upenn.edu	Yes	Yes	Yes		-	Yes	Yes	-	-
SU	hf.mrv@forsythe.stanford.edu	Yes	Yes	-		-	Yes	Yes	-	-
TU	No	-	-	-		-	-	-	-	-
WI	afrst@macc.wisc.edu	Yes	-	Yes	Eritrea-L Swahili-L Outreach Dirs	-	Yes	Yes	-	-
YU	No	Yes	Yes	-	Kamusi-L	No	No	No	-	-

Bib= Africana Bibliographer; LC= Language Coordinator; OD= Outreach Director

Universites = Boston University, University of California-Berkeley, University of California-Los Angeles, Columbia University, Central States University, University of Florida, Howard University, University of Illinois-Urbana/Champaign, Indiana University, University of Kansas, Lincoln University, Michigan State University, Ohio State University, Ohio University, University of Pennsylvania, Stanford University, Tuskegee University, University of Wisconsin-Madison, Yale University.

- = no person hired in the position or university does not provide service

[1]Not all the institutions provided complete information by the date of publication.

Internet resources for women's studies

Mary Glazier

As an interdisciplinary field, women's studies necessarily crosses into a wide number of overlapping subject areas. Though these distinctions were not always easy to make, I have undertaken the compilation of an introductory guide as a way of presenting sources that deal with the general relationship of women to various disciplines or that present women's perspectives on specific cultural institutions.

The following list of electronic resources for women's studies was created through the use of gophers, Archie, Veronica, and OPACs. Resources are divided into discussion groups (listservs precede Usenet groups), electronic journals, OPACs, electronic texts, fee-based services, gopher sites, and other resources indispensable for identifying listservs in any given subject area. It is my hope that, with the following resources as a starting point, women will be able to pursue their own interests and identify sources of information specific to their needs and that this guide will highlight areas where resources are needed (such as electronic journals) so that complete access to women's studies resources can become a reality.

Electronic mail discussion groups (listservs)

The following is a selective list of listservs on general topics relevant to women's studies. Generally, to subscribe, one should send the message "Subscribe firstname lastname" to the address indicated after *"Subscribe."*

Mary Glazier is reference/instruction librarian at the State University of New York at Buffalo; e-mail: mglazier@ubvm.cc.buffalo.edu

- EDUCOM-W is a moderated list to facilitate discussion of issues in technology and education that are of interest to women. *Subscribe:* LISTSERV@BITNIC.EDUCOM.EDU.
- FEMAIL is a moderated list which provides a shared communication channel for feminists around the world. Women and men are welcome to join. *Subscribe:* FEMAIL-REQUEST@LUCERNE.ENG.SUN.COM.
- FEMECON-L listserv for feminist economists. A source of information and answers to questions on economics with feminist perspectives. *Subscribe:* LISTSERV@BUCKNELL.EDU.
- FEMINISM-DIGEST. Issues of feminist organization, experience, and philosophy are discussed. This is a collation of the articles that appear on Usenet's SOC.FEMINISM list, sent out about once a week. *Subscribe:* Feminism-Digest@NCAR.UCAR.EDU.
- FEMINIST, owned by the Feminist Task Force of the American Library Association, offers discussions of issues such as sexism, racism, and ethnic diversity in librarianship and pornography, censorship, and intellectual freedom in libraries. LISTSERV@MITVMA.MIT.EDU
- FEMISA is a discussion of feminism, gender, women's international relations, world politics, the international political economy, and global politics. One of the purposes of the list is the exchange of documents (course outlines, articles, etc.) related to its topics. *Subscribe:* LISTSERV@CSF.COLORADO.EDU.
- FEMREL-L is a list providing a great deal of conversation about women, religion, and feminist theology. *Subscribe:* LISTSERV@UMCVMB.BITNET.
- FIST (feminism in science and technology) is an unmoderated list for discussion of feminism and science and technology. *Subscribe:* LISTSERV@DAWN.HAMPSHIRE.EDU.
- GENDER is a moderated list devoted especially to discussion of issues pertaining to the study of communication and gender. *Subscribe:* COSERVE@RPITSVM.
- H-WOMEN is an international forum for scholars and teachers of women's history. *Subscribe:* LISTSERV@UICVM.BITNET.
- KOL-ISHA is a moderated list for questions and issues concerning women's roles in Judaism. *Subscribe:* LISTSERV@ISRAEL.NYSERNET.ORG.
- MEDFEM-L is a list for feminist medievalists. *Subscribe:* LISTSERV@UWAVM.U.WASHINGTON.EDU.
- SWIP-L is an information and discussion list for Society for Women in Philosophy members and others interested in feminist philosophy. *Subscribe:* LISTSERV@CFRVM.CFR.USF.EDU.
- SYSTERS provides a forum for female computer scientists for the exchange of research and career information. Contact Anita Borg at SYSTERS-REQUEST@DECWRL.DEC.COM.

• WIM-L (Women's Issues in Music Librarianship). Contact Laura Gayle Green at LGREEN@IUBVM.BITNET.
• WIPHYS is a moderated list for issues of concern to women in physics. *Subscribe:* LISTSERV@NYSERNET.ORG.
• WISENET is a list for women in science, mathematics, and engineering. *Subscribe:* LISTSERV@UICVM.UIC.EDU.
• WMN-HLTH (women's health electronic news-line) was started by the Center for Women's Health Research. *Subscribe:* LISTSERV@UMDD. UMD.EDU.
• WMST-L serves academic and professional needs of people involved in women's studies teaching, research, libraries, and programs. *Subscribe:* LISTSERV@UMDD.UMD.EDU.
• WOMEN is a general purpose list for all women's groups and areas of interest for women and their friends. *Subscribe:* WOMEN-REQUEST@ ATHENA.MIT.EDU.

Usenet newsgroups
Methods of accessing Usenet newsgroups vary from system to system; the best approach is to ask your system administrator.
• ALT.FEMINISM is often a venue for confrontational debates about feminism.
• SOC.WOMEN offers an unrestricted range of topics, mostly nonacademic, of relevance to women's lives.
• SOC.GENDER-ISSUES is a discussion of gender issues of interest to women.
• SOC.FEMINISM is a moderated list where issues of feminist organization, experience, and philosophy are discussed. (Also available through the Internet as FEMINISM-DIGEST@NCAR.UCAR.EDU.)

Electronic journals
• AMAZONS INTERNATIONAL is an electronic journal for and about "physically and psychologically strong, assertive women who are not afraid to break free from traditional ideas about gender roles and femininity." Gopher to gopher.cic.net. Select "Electronic Serials." Select "General Subject Headings" then "Culture."

OPACs (online library catalogs)
The following OPACs offer access to library collections which are known for having strong women's studies collections. Most gopher systems provide access to library catalogs, however, telnet addresses are listed below for those who wish to connect directly to these catalogs. (*Note:* some systems

are not entirely compatible with telnet access; for some systems you may need to type TN3270 or TNVT100 instead of "telnet." If you are in doubt, check with the system administrator at your school to determine which command you should use.)
- BROWN. Telnet to BROWNVM.BROWN.EDU. At the BROWN logon screen: TAB to command field. Enter DIAL JOSIAH. TAB to the JOSIAH choice on the screen.
- NORTHWESTERN UNIVERSITY. Telnet to LIBRARY.UCC.NWU.EDU. At the Database Selection Menu, enter NCAT.
- TEXAS WOMAN'S UNIVERSITY. Telnet to VENUS.TWU.EDU. At the Username: prompt, type IRIS. Press RETURN several times when prompted.
- UNIVERSITY OF CALIFORNIA AT IRVINE (MELVYL). Telnet to MELVYL. UCOP.EDU. When asked for terminal type, enter VT100. Press RETURN when prompted. Type START LOOK for easy-to-use library system.
- UNIVERSITY OF NORTH CAROLINA AT GREENSBORO. Telnet to STEFFI. UNCG.EDU. When prompted for Username, type JACLIN.
- UNIVERSITY OF MARYLAND. Telnet to VICTOR.UMD.EDU. Select PAC from the Available Services Menu. Select 5 for VT100. Press RETURN twice.

Electronic texts
The Women Writers Project provides texts of some 200 literary works produced by women writers from pre-1830 England, Scotland, Ireland, and Wales. It also includes works from other colonies. The listserv (WWP-L) offers a forum for discussion of these works (*subscribe:* LISTSERV@ BROWNVM.BROWN.EDU).

Fee-based services
- WON, the Women's Online Network, was founded by Carmela M. Federico and Stacy M. Horn in January 1992 and is concerned with developing strategies to improve the position of women in our society. The network distributes prominent and essential information regarding concerns to women, and aids in the coordination of useful political action. Annual membership is $20, which is negotiable if necessary. To join, contact the cofounders at (212) 255-3839 or (212) 989-8411 or e-mail to carmela@echo.panix.com or horne@echo.panix.com.
- WIRE, Women's Information Resource and Exchange, due to begin operation in 1994, will be an international interactive computer network providing women with a centralized source of women-oriented information and conversation. For information contact WIRE at (415) 615-8989 or e-mail to info@uivc.net.

Gopher sites
• INFOGOPHER.YORK.AC.UK includes Internet guides as well as bibliographies on women's studies and feminism. Select "Library," then "Subjects," then "Women's Studies." The following guides are recommended and are available at this site under "Internet Guides:"

Balka, Ellen. *Women's Access to On-line Discussions about Feminism.*

Hunt, Laura. *Guide to Women's Studies/Feminist Information on the Internet.* 2nd ed.

Turek, Kathleen, and Judith Hudson. *Electronic Access to Research on Women: A Short Guide.*

• INFO.UMD.EDU. The University of Maryland's gopher, InForM, houses the Women's Studies Online Database. Divided by subject, it includes calls for papers, employment opportunities, feminist film reviews, women's health information, poetry, fiction, political information, and more. Select "Educational Resources," then "Women's Studies."

• HAFNHAF.MICRO.UMN.EDU The University of Minnesota Women's Center's gopher site offers access to information about counseling, education, family relations, health, finances, housing, research, violence, current events, scholarships, grants, financial support, and much more. Select "UofM Campus Information," then "University of Minnesota Women's Center."

Other Resources
• SOC.FEMINISM FAQ (Frequently Asked Questions) provides "an informal compilation of potential resources for women" and includes feminist organizations, related organizations, feminist and women-oriented publications, feminist and women-oriented electronic mailing lists, and a list of catalogs/bookstores. It is available through ftp to rtfm.mit.edu as "resources" under/pub/usenet/news.answers/feminism.

Reprinted from C&RL News, Vol. 55, No. 3, March 1994.

Internet resources for business

Leslie M. Haas

New sources are being added to the Internet daily, and many of us have a difficult time keeping track of what is out there in our subject area. One solution to this problem has been to create subject bibliographies of what is available and make them accessible via anonymous ftp and gophers to those who are interested.

Approximately a year ago, a question was posted on BUSLIB-L asking for help finding such a guide for business. On discovering that there wasn't one available, several librarians decided to create one. The result was Business *Sources on the Net* (*BSN*). Currently, *BSN* is divided into nine different files, each on a different business subject. There are plans to add new subjects as more sources become available on the Net and to update the existing files.

The files are available via anonymous ftp to ksuvxa.kent.edu in the *Library Directory* and also through the gopher at refmac.kent.edu 70 under the name *Business Sources on the Net*.

The resources available to business researchers are varied. The following are highlights from each of the files in the directory. Listed at the end of each section are the names of those persons responsible for putting that section together.

The connection information includes the protocol to be used (e.g., telnet, ftp) followed by the address of the host site and any subdirectories of login information. Example: Protocol//address/subdirectory/subdirectory.

Leslie M. Haas is the business reference librarian at the Kent State University Libraries, Ohio; e-mail: lhaas@kentvm.kent.edu

General business sources

The following resources are general business sources that will be useful to people in different areas of business. Sources in this section include: telephone books, current events, and government information.

• Small Business Bibliography. Gopher://gopher.fsu.edu/libraries/Strozier Library Research Guides/Topic or Alph List/Small Business Bibliography. A brief bibliography and "how to find" guide for small business clientele.

• Gross State Product Tables. Gopher://lib.umich.edu/Social Sciences Research/Economics. This database contains economic information on the state level.

• Washlaw. Telnet://acc.wuacc.edu. Login: washlaw. Information on this system includes: The 1993-94 U.S Budget, 1990 Census data, and Congressional bills. Users can search the system by types of law (commercial, intellectual property, disability, etc.) Washlaw also allows users to connect to other Internet tools.

• Fedworld Electronic Marketplace. Telnet://fedworld.gov/name/user-id. This resource is a gateway to many government bulletin boards which may include data sets. Two boards that may be of interest to business persons are: The Census Board and the GPO Bulletin Board. *Current Industrial Reports* and *Census Board News Releases* are just two of the sources that are accessible using these bulletin boards.—*Elizabeth B. Richmond, University of Wisconsin-Eau Claire; Lelah Lugo, University of Wisconsin-Stout; Michele McKnelly, University of Wisconsin-River Falls*

Economics

The following resources cover the area of economics.

• Economic Bulletin Board at the University of Michigan: UNA.HH. LIB.UMICH.EDU. This is by far one of the most important sources of economic data on the Internet. This site downloads approximately one third of all the files available on the Economic Bulletin Board. The information contained on this bulletin board is usually current textual information. It is available for both ftp and gopher file transfers.

• Sam Houston State University. Gopher://niord.shsu.edu/. Documents included at this gopher site include selected economic bibliographies and the text of the NAFTA documents.

• Federal Reserve Bank of Boston. Gopher://NEEEDC.UMESBS.MAINE. EDU/FRBB/. This bulletin board contains regional economic data from the Federal Reserve Bank of Boston. Both text and compressed files are available by ftp.

• CSEMLIST@HASARA11.BITNET. To subscribe send a message to saraserv@hasara11.bitnet with the line: "Subscribe CSEMLIST Your Name".

This list serves as an information distribution system for researchers in the field of computational economics.—*Carl Braun, Syracuse University*

Foreign statistics, economic trends, and international management
Foreign and international items in this section are defined from the U.S.'s perspective.
• 10 a.m. EST Foreign Exchange Rates. Gopher://una.hh.lib.umich.edu/ebb/monetary/tenfx.frb.
• Historic Price Data for U.K., U.S., Canada, Norway, and Sweden. Gopher://niord.shsu.edugopher_root:[_Data.Economics.Price].
• International Marketing Insights, C&E Europe. Gopher://nestroy.wewein.ac.at/1/pub/cerro/profiles. Reports by the U.S. embassies and consulates on important developments with trade and investment implications.
• Journal of the International Academy of Hospitality Research. To subscribe contact the editor/publisher at JIAHRED@VTM1.CC.VT.EDU. This journal publishes refereed articles on basic and applied research on aspects of hospitality and tourism. It is published by the Scholarly Communications Project of Virginia Polytechnic Institute and State University, Blacksburg.—*Mel Westerman and Gary White, Pennsylvania State University*

Finance and banking
Sources of information in the three areas of corporate finance are presented in this section: money, banking, and credit.
• National Bureau of Economic Research. FTP:/nber/harvard/edu//. These three files contain the *Survey of Consumer Finance.*
• New England Banking Data. FTP://neeedc.umesbs.maine.edu/edu/frbb/banking. These files contain information on the New England economy. Performance measures for banks in the New England area and financial statements are two of the files available from this site.
• E-Finance. To subscribe send a message to listserv@templevm with the line "Subscribe E-Finance Your first name Your last name". The *Electronic Journal of Financing* disseminates information of interest to academic researchers in finance.—*Jan Tudor, Willamette University; Theodora Haynes, Rutgers University; Shari Buxbaum, Michigan State University*

Human resources
Information on human resources/personnel management is available in this section. (*Note:* No benchmarking information or local human resources operations have been included in this file.)
• Human Resources and Industrial Psychology Section of the Directory of Scholarly Electronic Conferences. Gopher://gopher.uask.ca./Computing/

Internet Information/Directory of Scholarly Electronic Conferences/Business, Miscellaneous Academic and News/Human Resources and Industrial Psychology. Major discussion lists in the area of human resources and industrial psychology are listed in this section of the directory.
• Employment Statistics, U.S. Economic Bulletin Board. Gopher:// una.hh.lib.umich.edu/ebb/employment/*.*; ftp:/una.hh.lib.umich.edu/ebb/ employment/*.*; ftp://una.hh.lib.umich.edu/ebb/bin [binary transfer for larger files]. These files contain a variety of statistical and textual information on employment and labor. Some of the files available in the employment directory include: BLS Employment Cost Index, Employment Situation, civilian labor force and unemployment by state, household employment statistics, major collective bargaining settlement, average wage and compensation tables, and unemployment rates by state and selected industry divisions.
• HRIS-L@UALTVM.BITNET. To subscribe send a message to listserv@ualtvm with the line "Subscribe HRIS-L Your first name Your last name". Human Resources Information (Canada) E-Conference is for payroll, personnel, and administration employees. This list is moderated.—*Hope N. Tillman, Babson College; Gary White, Pennsylvania State University; Theo Haynes, Rutgers University*

Management science, statistical methods, and operations
Coverage of these topics has been combined because of the overlap in the resources available. (*Note:* Course descriptions are excluded from this listing.)
• Laboratory of Manufacturing Research, Working Paper, Faculty of Management, University of Toronto. Ftp://fmgmt.mgmt.utoronto.ca/*. The working papers are either forthcoming in specified journals or submitted for publication.
• CHANCE. Gopher://cameron.geom.umn.edu/CHANCE/*.*. This database contains material designed to be helpful in teaching a CHANCE course. CHANCE is a case study course based on current chance events as reported in the daily newspapers.
• MNF-STRATEGY@MAILBASE.AC.UK. To subscribe send a message to mailbase@mailbase.ac.uk with the line "join MNF-STRATEGY Your first name Your last name". The Manufacturing Strategy is a forum for researchers and practitioners in the fields of manufacturing strategy formulation and performance measurement system design.
• SCI.OP-RESEARCH. This Usenet Newsgroup is the umbrella group for the operations research/management community. Focus is on research, application, and teaching.—*Hope N. Tillman, Babson College; Perry Horner and Terry Meyer, Arizona State University; Ann Scholz, University of Wisconsin-Parkside*

Accounting and taxation

The main sources of information available in the area of accounting and taxation come from the General Accounting Office (GAO). The GAO is an investigative arm of Congress that examines issues concerning the receipt and disbursement of public funds.

• Wiretap Internet. Gopher://wiretap.spies.com/gov. This site contains GAO publications including *GAO High Risk Reports, GAO Technical Reports,* and *GAO Miscellaneous Reports.*

• Villanova Tax Law Compendium. Gopher://ming.law.vill.edu/.taxlaw./. This is a collection of student tax papers available to students and practitioners through the Villanova gopher.

• CapAccess. Telnet://cap.gwu.edu/go federal/Legislative Branch Menu. Logon: Guest. Password: Visitor. The National Capital Area Public Access Network in cooperation with GAO is providing access to the *GAO Daybook.* The *Daybook* lists the current daily reports and testimony by the GAO.

• FEDTAX-L@SHSU. To subscribe send a message to listserv@shsu with the line "subscribe FEDTAX-L Your first name Your last name". This unmoderated discussion list focuses on both the practical and academic viewpoints of various federal taxation issues.—*Barbara Mento, Boston College; Sharmon Kenyon, Humboldt State University; Wendy Diamond, University of California, Berkeley; Barbara Butler, University of Nevada, Reno*

Management including public and nonprofit organizations

Concentration in this section is on sources of management information in organizational behavior, organization theory, management of new and small business, corporate and strategic planning, and the management of public and nonprofit organizations.

• The Management Archive (University of Minnesota). Gopher:// chimera.sph.umn.edu. The Archives provide access to contributed papers and preprints in the management and organizational sciences, recent paper calls, course syllabi, teaching materials, etc.

• CNI-MANAGEMENT@CNI.ORG. To subscribe send a message to listserv@cni.org with the line "subscribe CNI-MANAGEMENT Your first name Your last name". This forum is for those interested in issues about the training and education of management professionals.

• ESBDC-L@FERRIS. To subscribe send a message to listserv@ferris with the line "subscribe ESBDC-L Your first name Your last name". This unmoderated discussion group is aimed at facilitating discussion among small business development centers.—*Jan Tudor and Sridhar Krishan, Willamette University; Theodora Haynes, Rutgers University*

Computers

This section focuses on computers as they relate to the general area of business. (*Note:* Excluded in this section are course descriptions, local operations, and files that are specific to a brand of hardware or software.)

• Computer Science and Related Areas section of the *Directory of Scholarly Electronic Conferences*. Gopher://gopher.usask.ca/Computing/Internet Information/Directory of Scholarly Electronic Conferences/Computer Science and Related Areas. Computer conferences of the well-networked computer scientist community.

• *Art of Technology Digest*. Ftp://ftp.wuarchive.wustl.edu/doc/misc/aot/*. This journal is devoted to sharing information among computerists and to the presentation and debate of diverse views.

• Computing Electronic Serials. Gopher://gopher.cic.net/e-serials/general/computing. A variety of titles are represented including: *Apple, Interpersonal Computing and Technology,* and *Computer Networking Journals.— Hope Tillman, Babson College*

Investment information

There has always been keen interest in investment data via the Internet. The following sources focus on those sources that are of interest to the individual investor. (*Note:* As with paper sources, interest may wane and the source could disappear.)

• E Mail Quoter. Ftp://ftp.dg-rtp.dg.com/pub/misc.invest/quote dump. Contains selected daily prices and market oscillator readings. Data is also ranked by advances, declines, percent change and a variety of other measures. (*Note:* Information is deemed reliable, but never guaranteed.)

• Financial Economics Network (AFA_FIN). Send a message to MARRM@CLEMSON.EDU (Wayne Marr) or TRIMBLE@VANCOUVER.WSU. EDU (John Trimble) to subscribe to this service. AFA_FIN contains eleven moderated lists on a variety of topics including real estate, banking, international finance, and investments.—*Pearl Alberts, O'Neill Library*

Reprinted from C&RL News, Vol. 55, No. 4, April 1994.

Internet resources for distance education

Rob Morrison and Jill H. Ellsworth

Introduction

The Internet is full of resources for those interested in Distance Education. As with all subjects, information can be obtained using Internet search tools such as Gopher, Veronica, Jughead, and WAIS. Using Distance Education/ learning and adult education/learning, these searches will reveal many interesting documents, sites and databases on the constantly changing net.

J. H. Ellsworth maintains a list called "Dr. E's Eclectic Compendium of Electronic Resources for Adult/Distance Education." This resource is available as part of the University of Michigan's Clearinghouse for Subject-Oriented Internet Resources Guides. Current access is through anonymous FTP and Gopher. (FTP host: una.hh.lib.umich.edu, path: /inetdirs, file: disted: ellsworth)

For the purpose of this article, distance education is defined as any education taking place at a distance where a geographical separation exists between the instructor and the learner.

Discussion Lists

There are several scholarly and general discussion lists explicitly focussed ondistance education, as well as a number of educational lists which touch on DE regularly.

Rob Morrison is the Distance Education Library Services Coordinator, Merrill Library at Utah State University, e-mail: robmor@cc.usu.edu; Jill H. Ellsworth is an assistant professor at Southwest Texas State University. e-mail: je01@academia.swt.edu

•ADLTED-L. The Canadian Adult Education Network provides a forum for discussions worldwide. To subscribe, send message to: LISTSERV@UREGINA1.bitnet

•DEOS-L. The Distance Education Online Symposium List. Sponsored by the American Center for the Study of Distance Education (ACSDE) at Pennsylvania State University. Forum promotes discussion of distance education issues worldwide. The Center also produces a newsletter called DEOSNEWS. To subscribe, send the message: SUB DEOS-L Your Full Name to: LISTSERV@PSUVM.BITNET or to: LISTSERV@PSUVM.PSU.EDU

•EDISTA. Operated by the University Distance program (UNIDIS) at the University of Santiago in Chile. To subscribe, send the message: SUBSCRIBE EDISTA "your_full_name" to: LISTSERV@USACHVM1.BITNET Messages to the list can be sent via Bitnet: EDISTA@USACHVM1.BITNET

•EDNET. Operated by UMASS/Amherst, this list provides a forum for educators at all levels to discuss the educational possibilities of electronic communication and the Internet. To subscribe, send the message: subscribe EDNET Your Name to: listproc@lists.umass.edu

•SATEDU-L. A Satellite Educators list intended to exchange information and discuss issues of interest to satellite educators. Discussion topics are limited to satellites, space, and education. Questions can be sent to the list owner, Deborah Economidis, DelValnet Intern, Educational Center for Earth, Observational Systems, West Chester University. E-mail: DMartin@wcu.bitnet or DMartin@mainvm.wcupa.edu. To subscribe, send message: SUBSCRIBE SATEDU-L Firstname Lastname to: LISTSERV@WCU.BITNET or to: LISTSERV@MAINVM.WCUPA.EDU

Library Discussion Lists
•DISTLIB-L. Open discussion list for those interested in the development of librarians and library services in Canada. Sponsored by the Services for Distance Learning Interest Group of the Canadian Library Association. To subscribe, send the message: SUBSCRIBE DISTLIB-L firstname lastname to: LISTSERV@LIB.LAKEHEADU.CA

•OFFCAMP. Established by Wayne State University to provide an open forum to discuss issues concerning library services to remote users. To subscribe, send message: subscribe OFFCAMP firstname lastname to: LISTSERV@WAYNEST1.BITNET or to: LISTSERV@CMS.CC.WAYNE.EDU

Conference Directories
•The Directory of Scholarly Electronic Conferences is produced by Kent State University and accessible through many gophers. This database contains descriptions of electronic conferences by subject and includes discussion

lists, newsgroups, interest-groups, electronic journals and newsletters. To access, conduct a veronica search using "scholarly."

Electronic Journals and Newsletters
These are some electronic journals and newsletters that are of particular interest to Distance Educators.

• DEOSNEWS. The Distance Education Online Symposium News. Produced by the ASCDE. An international electronic journal. To subscribe, send the message: SUB DEOSNEWS Your Full Name to: LISTSERV@PSUVM.BITNET or to: LISTSERV@PSUVM.PSU.EDU

• DISTED. The Online Journal of Distance Education and Communication from the University of Alaska. Articles focus on four content areas: Distance Education, Distance Communication, Telecommunications in Education, and Cross-Cultural Communication. To subscribe, send the message: SUB DISTED your_full_name to: LISTSERV@UWAVM. A subscription will provide references to articles which can be retrieved directly from the Listserv or via anonymous FTP.

• INFOBITS. A service provided by the Institute for Academic Technology's Information Resources Group. Current newsletter for college and university educators distributing selective sources in information technology and instruction technology. This is a moderated list. To subscribe, send the following message: SUBSCRIBE INFOBITS firstname lastname to: listserv@gibbs.oit.unc.edu

• IPCT. Interpersonal Computing and Technology: An Electronic Journal for the 21st Century. Published by the Center for Teaching and Technology, Academic Computing Center at Georgetown University. Peer-reviewed articles on the use of computers and other electronic communication systems used in higher education. To subscribe, send the message: SUBSCRIBE IPCT-J YOURFIRSTNAME YOURLASTNAME to: LISTSERV@GUVM.GEORGETOWN.EDU or to: LISTSERV@GUVM

• JTE-L. Journal of Technology Education. Produced by the Technology Education Program, Virginia Polytechnic Institute and State University. This journal contains peer-reviewed articles focusing on the use of technology in education. To subscribe, send the message: SUBSCRIBE JTE-L firstname lastname to: LISTSERV@VTVM1.CC.VT.EDU or to: LISTSERV@VTVM1 A list of all files can be obtained by sending the message INDEX JTE-L to: LISTSERV@VTVM1

• JOE. Journal of Extension published by the University of Wisconsin. Refereed publication of the Cooperative Extension System, covers Extension and Adult Education issues. Full-text articles are available directly from the listserv or via anonymous FTP. To subscribe, send the message: subscribe joe to: almanac@joe.uwex.edu

Databases
There are some special databases of interest in DE.
• ERIC. Provides a rich repository of educationally related papers, studies, reports and information, has abundant DE materials, and can be reached through Syracuse University, the University of Maryland, Auburn University, CARL and many other libraries and gopher servers. ASKERIC is a service that will provide answers to education-related questions. Send a message to: ASKERIC@ERICIR.SYR.EDU or telnet to the gopher: ERICIR.SYR.EDU
• The International Centre for Distance Learning (ICDL). Based at the British Open University, has a large online database on Distance Education. This database has been developed with funding from the British Government's Overseas Development Administration to provide an information service to the Commonwealth of Learning (based in Canada), an organization created by Commonwealth Heads of Government to expand opportunities for students in Commonwealth countries through distance education. There are three sections in the database: Courses, Institutions, and Literature. There are costs associated with the use of this database; it can be accessed from the Internet using Telnet:

> telnet sun.nsf.ac.uk or telnet 128.86.8.7
> login: janet (lower case)
> password: ICDL
> host name: uk.ac.janet.news

• The Cleveland Free-net (Telnet to freenet-in-a.cwru.edu and register as a visitor unless you have an account). Archives the papers and scholarly list transcripts from what is known as the Bangkok Distance Learning Conference (The International Conference on Distance Education,November 6-8, 1992, Sukhothai Thammathirat Open University, Bangkok, Thailand) which generated a great deal of interest on the nets as it was taking place. The archives can be found in the Usenet news section of the Free-net. The Usenet can be accessed from The Teleport section from the main directory. Then select "Complete Usenet Groups" to access the Usenet DE Archival files:

> alt.education.bangkok
> alt.education.bangkok.cmc
> alt.education.bangkok.databases
> alt.education.bangkok.planning
> alt.education.bangkok.research
> alt.education.bangkok.student
> alt.education.bangkok.theory
> alt.education.distance.

In addition, in alt.education.distance some of the topics currently include the National Instructional Satellite Service, the Davenport Media Literacy Program, distance learning programs in Physics, GED materials, computer mediated distance learning, the University of Phoenix distance learning degree programs, copyrights and distance learning, and more. As with most archives and usenet lists, the material changes day-to-day.

Other resources include:

• The National Project for Computer-based Distance Education at Miami Dade Community College.

• The National Distance Learning Center at Owensboro Community College in Kentucky. Assists in distributing and accessing courseware for distance education program producers and users. To access, telnet to: NDLC.OCC.UKY. EDU or: 128.163.193.10 Login: ndlc

• The Centre for Distance Education at Athabasca University is creating a database of email addresses of adult and distance education researchers in an effort to provide information and connections.

Reprinted from C&RL News, Vol. 55, No. 5, May 1994. Revised January, 1995.

Internet resources for engineering

Thomas P. Dowling

The Internet, with its ability to link countless users to each other and to information resources, excels at providing very current information. Engineering, with its need to coordinate current research, excels at using very current information. Not surprisingly, it turns out that there are many sources of engineering information on the Internet.

Lists and newsgroups

A large number of lists and newsgroups carry engineering information. The most complete directory of mailing lists is the *Directory of Scholarly Electronic Conferences*. Of particular interest are sections 6 (physical sciences) and 8 (computer science). To retrieve the most current version of the directory, either send mail to listserv@kentvm.kent.edu with no subject and with the two lines "get acadlist file6 / get acadlist file8" as the body of the message, or use anonymous ftp to get the files from ksuvxa.kent.edu in the library directory.

One list which does not show up in these sections of the directory is ELDNET-L, the list for the Engineering Libraries Division of the American Society for Engineering Education. To subscribe, send e-mail to listserv@vmd.cso.uiuc.edu with the single line "subscribe eldnet-l <firstname lastname>".

Many engineers rely heavily on Usenet newsgroups. While the specific newsgroups available vary from site to site, most groups related to

Thomas P. Dowling is engineering computer-based services librarian at the University of Washington, Seattle; e-mail: tdowling@lib.washington.edu

engineering will be commonly available. Especially helpful will be groups in the hierarchies of sci.engr (sci.engr, sci.engr.biomed, sci.engr.chem, sci.engr.civil, sci.engr.control, sci.engr.manufacturing, sci.engr.mech), sci.space (sci.space, sci.space.news, sci.space.policy, sci.space.science, sci.space.shuttle, sci.space.tech), and ieee (ieee.announce, ieee.general) and the groups comp.rg.ieee, comp.org.acm, sci.aeronautics, and misc.books.technical.

Databases of interest

A number of specialized databases are available on the Internet with implications for engineers. Some of these are either databases of special library collections, or are available through library catalogs, and others are available as separate services.

• Buckyballs. The University of Arizona's online library catalog provides access to the Buckyball database, a bibliographic database on the literature of buckminsterfullerenes, a family of carbon molecules with implications for research in chemical engineering and superconductivity.

To use the database, telnet to sabio.arizona.edu. Press O (the letter "o," not zero) to use other databases, and then enter 1 for the buckyball database.

Technical reports

• Stanford Technical Reports Database. One of the chronically difficult challenges in using engineering literature is finding technical reports. Stanford University's online library catalog offers a connection to the Stanford database of technical reports. The database provides keyword searching by author, organization, title, subject, and report or contract number.

To use the database, telnet to forsythetn.stanford.edu and login with the account "socrates". At the response prompt, enter "select technical reports". To exit, enter the command "end" at any prompt.

Full-text reports via gopher

A growing number of universities and corporations are making the full text of their technical reports available online. Most frequently, they are distributed via gopher servers in PostScript format. While these gopher servers are themselves scattered around the entire Internet, a server at the University of South Carolina provides pointers to them; the server is at gopher. math.scarolina.edu, port 70, under the menu choice labelled "Distributed Multi-Topic Infor Resources."

Another important set of technical reports available via the Net is at NASA's Langley Research Center; it is available for anonymous ftp at techreports. larc.nasa.gov in the /pub/techreports/larc directory. These reports have recently been made available for searching via the World Wide Web (WWW) at http://mosaic.larc.nasa.gov/ltrs/ltrs.html.

Government information

• EPA. The Environmental Protection Agency (EPA) offers an Internet connection to several of its databases, including its national library catalog, a database of hazardous waste materials, the Access EPA database of directory information, and several others. To use the service, telnet to epaibm. rtpnc.epa.gov. Enter 4 for public applications, then 1 for the library system, and then optionally enter your name.

• STIS. The National Science Foundation's (NSF) Science and Technology Information System (STIS) provides information about NSF awards, programs, guidelines for proposals, publications, and other information. STIS provides connections via telnet; telnet to stis.nsf.gov, login as "public", and enter "new" to register as a new user. STIS is also available as a gopher server at stis.nsf.gov, port 70.

• NASA. SCAN. Selected Current Aerospace Notices (SCAN), NASA's current-awareness bibliographies, are available online in several formats. They are available via a listserv (send the message "lists" to listserv@sti.nasa.gov— be aware that SCAN can generate a lot of e-mail); they are available via gopher at gopher.sti.nasa.gov, port 70; and they are available via WWW at http://www.sti.nasa.gov/scan.html.

• NASA. RECON. As of this writing, NASA is providing access to three years' worth of its RECON database. Citations from *International Aerospace Abstracts* and from *Scientific and Technical Aerospace Reports* can be searched by keyword. This is available within WWW at http://www. sti.nasa.gov/recon-wais.html.

• Other NASA WWW servers. NASA maintains a number of other WWW resources; the NASA home page is at http://hypatia.gsfc.nasa.gov/ NASA_homepage.html. Links to servers at the Kennedy Space Center provide a large amount of technical information on space shuttle missions, and historical information on NASA space flight missions.

• Fedworld. Fedworld is a bulletin board system run by the National Technical Information Service (NTIS). Telnet to fedworld.gov; you will need to register to use the service. In addition to the Fedworld information itself, there are gateways to over a hundred other federal bulletin boards, ranging in coverage from defense conversion to rules for decommissioning nuclear power plants to offshore oil and gas data. Many of these bulletin boards will also require you to register as a user.

• National Institute of Standards and Technology (NIST). NIST maintains a WWW server at http://www.nist.gov/welcome.html which leads to information on NIST programs, including the Malcolm Baldridge National Quality Award, and descriptions of research at NIST laboratories.

Standards

A small number of services are starting to provide information about industry standards via the Internet. Document Center provides a free index for searching its document delivery inventory by standard number. Subscribers can also search by keyword and place delivery orders online. In addition, Document Center is planning to add the full text of standards from participating industry and government organizations. Document Center's WWW server is at http://doccenter.com/doccenter/home.html.

Professional organizations

A number of engineering organizations are providing information via the Internet, especially through gopher servers.

• Association for Computing Machinery: includes a calendar of forthcoming conferences, calls for papers, publication lists, and membership services (gopher.acm.org, port 70).

• Institute of Electrical and Electronics Engineers (IEEE): includes membership and chapter information (gopher.ieee.org, port 70).

• IEEE Computer Society: includes calls for papers, membership information, and tables of contents for society publications (info.computer.org, port 70).

• Society of Industrial and Applied Mathematics: includes advance conference programs and calls for papers, and book reviews (gopher.siam.org, port 70).

Guides and updates

A number of electronic sources are tracking engineering information on the networks. As the rate at which information sources become available online increases, the online sources for tracking them will be able to keep pace more reliably than print guides.

• Engineering Virtual Library. This is a subject guide to WWW sources. The recent explosive growth in Mosaic applications makes this guide increasingly important; it is available at http://epims1.gsfc.nasa.gov/engineering/engineering.html.

• Library Without Walls. North Carolina State University's gopher server, the Library Without Walls includes subject guides to many disciplines including engineering. It is located at dewey.lib.ncsu.edu, port 70, in the "Library Without Walls/Study Carrels" menu.

- InfoSlug. The University of California-Santa Cruz maintains a gopher server named InfoSlug which includes a subject guide to research materials. It is at scilibx.ucsc.edu, port 70, in the "The Researcher" menu.
- University of Michigan SILS. The University of Michigan School of Information and Library Studies (SILS) has created several thorough subject guides to Internet resources, including aerospace engineering and environment issues. These are available at una.hh.lib.umich.edu, port 70, in the "inetdirs" directory.
- EINet Galaxy. EINet Galaxy provides a guide to many engineering sources via the WWW. The guide is available at http://galaxy.einet.net/galaxy/Engineering-and-Technology.html.

Reprinted from C&RL News, Vol. 55, No. 6, June 1994. Revised January, 1995.

Internet resources for English and American literature

Loss Pequeño Glazier

Numerous academic disciplines have felt the influence of the Internet, English and American literature studies among them. Perhaps in no other discipline, however, has the effect of the Internet been as intriguing, multifaceted, and theoretically relevant as in literary studies. In addition to facilitating discussions in the discipline, making texts available, and providing a medium for the publication of writing and research results, the Internet has even further-reaching implications for literary studies since electronic texts, in their various forms, have emerged as subjects themselves of literary investigations. Not only has this relevance of the electronic text provided a partial enactment of contemporary literary theory but electronic technologies have, as literary agencies, opened new methodologies in literary research.

The degree to which literary endeavors can be tied to technology (few no longer write without a word processor, as a very basic example) makes a list of Internet resources for English and American literature studies considerably challenging. For instance, for most humanities and social sciences disciplines electronic mail discussion groups (listservs) determine a fundamental level of scholarly interchange, with the more technologically engaged disciplines producing electronic journals. (If anyone needs reassurance about the scholarly validity of electronic journals, the recent acquisition

Loss Pequeño Glazier is English & American literature subject specialist at Lockwood Library, State University of New York at Buffalo; e-mail: LOLPOET@ UBVM.CC.BUFFALO.EDU

of the electronic *Postmodern Culture* by Oxford University Press is particularly worthy of note.)

Like most humanities and social sciences disciplines, English and American literature studies is clearly grounded in both of these forms of Internet exchange (with wildfires of electronic journals for creative work), but finds itself on even more intriguing terrain—sites dedicated to the circulation of electronic texts. A truly productive exploration of this discipline must begin with the knowledge that it is the intersection of these three areas of exchange that defines how the evolution of literary studies is manifest in English and American literature studies on the Internet.

The following resource list, therefore, aims to be diverse enough to represent different Internet areas; it must be selective because of the sheer amount of material available; and its goal is to be broad enough to recognize both the presence of interdisciplinary interests (such as the direct relation of certain philosophers to literary studies) and the larger arena of general humanities computing which offers resources indispensable to the student or scholar working in English and American literature studies.

It is my hope that this list will chart a context for English and American literature studies as available through the Internet and foster not only greater access to these sources but a more widespread understanding of immersion of the literary endeavor in this technology.

Electronic mail discussion groups (listservs)

Given the large number of candidates for this category, the following list of listservs relevant to English and American literature studies must by necessity be a highly selective one; choices were not always easy to make but the selections below aim to represent a "scholarly" level of discourse in the discipline. Numerous lists treating less canonical topics are not included because of space limitations. (Note that when both Internet and Bitnet addresses were available for a given list, the Internet address is provided here as more widely accessible.)

National literatures, genre, period, and literary theory

- AMLIT-L. American Literature Discussion List. Informal and often chatty discussion on various topics in American literature, frequently about themes and motifs (women performers, ghost stories, etc.). *Subscribe:* LISTSERV@MIZZOU1.MISSOURI.EDU.
- CHICLE. Chicano literature discussion group. Wide-ranging discussions in this generally under-represented area. *Subscribe:* LISTSERV@UNMVMA.UNM.EDU.
- LITERARY. This is a very active list on numerous general topics in literature and reading. *Subscribe:* LISTSERV@UCF1VM.CC.UCF.EDU.

- LITSCI-L. Society for Literature and Science. Issues related to literature, science, and technological literary culture. *Subscribe:* LISTSERV@VMD.CSO. UIUC.EDU.
- NATIVE-LIT-L. Discussion of literature of "autochthonous peoples of the North Americas (the U.S., Canada, and Mexico) and neighboring islands, including Hawaii." *Subscribe:* LISTSERV@CORNELL.EDU.
- PMC-TALK. A discussion list for the electronic journal *Postmodern Culture* featuring postmodern issues and news, announcements, and events of interest to scholars and writers. Subscription to PMC-TALK must be undertaken independently of a subscription to the journal. *Subscribe:* LISTSERV@LISTSERV.NCSU.EDU.
- VICTORIA. 19th-century British culture and society. This very active list on topics related to Victorian culture has a strong emphasis on literature. *Subscribe:* LITSERV@IUBVM.UCS.INDIANA.EDU.
- WWP-L. Under the aegis of the Brown University Women Writer's Project, this is an informational vehicle for discussion of Project texts. See also the entry under Electronic Texts. *Subscribe:* LISTSERV@BROWNVM.BROWN. EDU.

Single-author lists

The following lists offer forums for discussing the works and lives of individual authors. Most lists also disseminate queries, conference announcements, calls for papers, and information on new publications related to the author.

- AUSTEN-L covers Jane Austen and her contemporaries (e.g., Fanny Burney, Maria Edgeworth, and Mary Wollstonecraft). *Subscribe:* LISTSERV@MUSICA. MCGILL.CA.
- BRONTE on majordomo@world.std.com. covers Emily, Charlotte, and Anne Bronte. *Subscribe:* MAJORDOMO@WORLD.STD.COM (Note: Address subscription request to majordomo not listserv. Request should read subscribe bronte in the body of the e-mail message. Do not include your name after the list name.)
- CHAUCER covers Geoffrey Chaucer and medieval English Literature. *Subscribe:* LISTSERV@VTVM1.CC.VT.EDU.
- DICKNS-L covers Charles Dickens and offers access to files containing related bibliographies, papers, and articles from *Dickens' World. Subscribe:* LISTSERV@UCSBVM.UCSB.EDU.
- FWAKE-L covers James Joyce's *Finnegan's Wake* with general discussion of the novel and attention to "the jokes in *Finnegan's Wake.*" *Subscribe:* LISTSERV@IRLEARN.UCD.IE.
- JACK-LONDON covers the writings and political activism of Jack London. *Subscribe:* JACK-LONDON-REQUEST@SONOMA.EDU.

- MILTON-L covers John Milton. *Subscribe:* MILTON-REQUEST@URVAX. URICH.EDU.
- SHAKSPER. "SHAKSPER offers announcements and bulletins, scholarly papers, and the formal exchange of ideas—but it also offers ongoing opportunities for spontaneous informal discussion, eavesdropping, peer review, and a fresh sense of worldwide scholarly community." It also offers access to numerous related electronic files. *Subscribe:* LISTSERV@VM. UTCC.UTORONTO.CA.
- TROLLOPE covers Anthony Trollope. *Subscribe:* TROLLOPE@WORLD. STD.COM (*Note:* Address subscription request to majordomo not listserv. Request should read subscribe trollope in the body of the e-mail message. Do not include your name after the list name.)
- TWAIN-L covers Mark Twain. *Subscribe:* LISTSERV@VM1.YORKU.CA.

Philosophers relevant to literary studies
Philosophy, to varying degrees, has become inseparable from literary studies. (Perhaps the most salient example of this interdisciplinary activity is Jacques Derrida.) Representative examples of discussion groups that might be of interest to literary scholars include ADORNO (Theodor Adorno), BAUDRILLARD (Jean Baudrillard), and DELEUZE (Gilles Deleuze), all at THINKNET@WORLD.STD.COM and DERRIDA (Jacques Derrida and deconstruction) at LISTSERV@CFRVM.CFR.USF.EDU; HEGEL (G. W. F. Hegel, 1770–1831), the Hegel Society of America at LISTSERV@VILLVM.BITNET; KANT-L (Immanuel Kant) at LISTSERV@BUCKNELL.EDU.

Lists about writing
- CREWRT-L. Creative Writing Pedagogy for Teachers and Students. This is an extremely active list on topics related to the teaching of creative writing and its place in the college and university curriculum. *Subscribe:* LISTSERV@ MIZZOU1.MISSOURI.EDU.
- FICTION. Fiction Writers Workshop. It gives "people interested in writing fiction professionally a support group of peers." All list members are required to offer critiques of submitted writing in order to remain on the list. *Subscribe:* LISTSERV@PSUVM.PSU.EDU.
- MBU-L. Megabyte University. This is a list concerned with computers, composition, theoretical issues in writing instruction, and technology in the writing classroom. *Subscribe:* LISTSERV@TTUVM1.TTU.EDU.
- NOUS REFUSE. A writing collective for experimental poets moderated by Joe Amato, this list is very interesting, energetic, offbeat, and always willing to entertain new issues. For information contact JAMATO@UX1.CSO.UIUC. EDU.

- RPOETIK. Realpoetik is a moderated list where subscribers may submit material for distribution or comment. *Subscribe:* LISTSERV@WLN.COM.
- WRITERS is for professional writers and those who aspire to be writers. It is a busy list on the "craft" of writing but also on "the Oscars, the lunchboxes we had as kids, buttered cats and gravity, Tori Amos and whether *Picket Fences* and *Northern Exposure* are too similar." *Subscribe:* LISTSERV@VM1. NODAK.EDU.

Other relevant lists
- GUTNBERG is a mailing list for Project Gutenberg. See Electronic Texts section below. *Subscribe:* LISTSERV@VMD.CSO.UIUC.EDU.
- E-GRAD. This list is for graduate students in English and the modern languages sponsored by the Graduate Student Caucus of the Modern Language Association. *Subscribe:* LISTSERV@RUTVM1.RUTGERS.EDU.
- ETEXTCTR features discussion about all aspects of the development of electronic text centers. See Electronic Texts section below. *Subscribe:* LISTSERV@RUTVM1.RUTGERS.EDU.
- HUMANIST is the major list for those interested in humanities computing. It contains much information of relevance to those working in English and American literature studies. *Subscribe:* LISTSERV@BROWNVM.BROWN. EDU.
- TACT-L is a list for discussion of TACT, "Textual Analysis Computing Tools." It is a text-retrieval and analysis system of MS-DOS programs, developed at the Centre for Computing in the Humanities, University of Toronto. TACT-L also includes announcements of new research, publications, and courses involving TACT. *Subscribe:* LISTSERV@EPAS.UTORONTO.CA.

Usenet newsgroups
Methods of accessing Usenet newsgroups vary widely by system; to find out how you can access these groups, contact your system administrator. Usenet groups related to English and American literature studies, mostly with an emphasis on writing include ALT.BOOKS.REVIEWS, REC.ARTS. INT-FICTION, REC.ARTS.POEMS, REC.ARTS.PROSE, AND MISC.WRITING.

Electronic journals
Although traditional literary studies journals do not seem to have migrated to the Internet, there is no lack of electronic journals devoted to creative expression. A number of gophers now carry selected electronic journals but the challenge for a scholar who wishes to garner a sense of what kinds of literary activity are present is in for quite a bit of active digging. Journals may be accessed either through an archive (two major repositories of

electronic journals have emerged to date) or, in many cases, through a direct "subscription" to the journal.

Collections of electronic journals

• CICNET is a major repository for electronic journals. Be prepared to look in different menus for the journal you seek and keep in mind that no one archive contains all electronic journals. Gopher to GOPHER.CIC.NET and select "Electronic Serials" under the CICNet root menu.

• MICHIGAN ELECTRONIC TEXT ARCHIVE is a very complete archive that includes a lot of electronic journals not found elsewhere. Literary journals appear in several categories. Be sure to consult "Fiction," "Poetry," and also "Zines." Gopher to ETEXT.ARCHIVE.UMICH.EDU or FIR.CIC.NET.

Electronic journals

Interestingly, journals of new writing and new critical approaches have taken a strong foothold on the Internet. Of these, a few have risen to dominate the field. The following is intended to offer an introduction to this exciting new area of publishing. (Periodicals typified by declarative style rather than formal innovation, "zines," are not included here as the aim of this list is to offer "literary" suggestions.)

• *FICTION-ONLINE* is a new electronic fiction journal begun in June. To subscribe contact Bill Ramsay at NGWAZI@CLARK.NET.

• *GRIST ON-LINE* is "a new journal of electronic network poetry, art and culture." Edited by a publisher with long-standing credibility in the literary community, it publishes new and reissued work by established and emerging authors. Send e-mail to John Fowler at FOWLER@PHANTOM.COM.

• *INTER\FACE* is published at the State University of New York at Albany in an effort to offer an "open forum for the publication and distribution of creative work." For more information, send e-mail to bh4781@RACHEL.ALBANY.EDU.

• *POSTMODERN CULTURE* (PMC-LIST) is a peer-reviewed journal containing essays on postmodernist literary and social issues. It includes a popular culture column, news, and reviews on an intriguing selection of new books. Subscription is independent of the discussion list (see above) associated with the journal. *Subscribe:* LISTSERV@LISTSERV.NCSU.EDU.

• *RIF/T* features poetry, creative prose, and critical writing from contributors like Charles Bernstein, Robert Kelly, and many others disseminated through the E-POETRY list. Forthcoming volumes include a collection of work on Charles Olson and a Latin American poetry in translation issue. See also "E-Poetry Center" below. *RIF/T* is published through the E-Poetry listserv. To subscribe to the journal, you must subscribe to E-Poetry at LISTSERV@UBVM.CC.BUFFALO.EDU.

- *TREE.* TapRoot Reviews Electronic Edition offers brief but engaging reviews of "Independent, Underground, and Experimental language-centered arts" publications as appearing in *TapRoot Reviews* magazine. The June issue (#5) included about 300 reviews. Contact editor Luigi-Bob Drake at AU462@CLEVELAND.FREENET.EDU.
- *WE MAGAZINE* is a poetry journal now in its 17th volume. It is edited by a collective that includes editors in Santa Cruz, the Bay Area, New York City, and Albany. For more information, e-mail to CF2785@ALBNYVMS.BITNET.

Electronic text projects and archives

The electronic text projects and archives presented in this section take different approaches to providing access to electronic texts. Selections of texts vary according to the mission and inclination of an individual archive; overlap of material among them is not uncommon. These archives do seem to share the goal of making information freely available. Certainly, as the following list suggests, an immense amount of material is readily accessible. (Note: A new Internet-accessible directory of electronic text centers was slated to be made available by the end of June. For more information on this directory, contact Mary Mallery at MALLERY@EDEN.RUTGERS.EDU. You may also wish to subscribe to ETEXTCTR (see entry above) for information on developments in the field.

- CPET. The Catalogue of Projects in Electronic Text provides information on over 300 electronic text projects worldwide (but not the texts themselves) and is available at GOPHER.GEORGETOWN.EDU. First choose "The Catalogue of Projects in Electronic Text (CPET)" then "Digests Organized by Discipline" then "Literature" then "English - Literature."
- ELECTRONIC TEXT CENTER & ON-LINE ARCHIVE OF ELECTRONIC TEXTS. Alderman Library, University of Virginia. Although most of the resources here are not available to the general public, the center is a model for library-sponsored electronic text centers. For information, e-mail ETEXT@VIRGINIA.EDU.
- INTERNET WIRETAP. Available at WIRETAP.SPIES.COM, this is an extraordinary selection of resources, most notably in the menus "Electronic Books at Wiretap" and "Various ETEXT Resources on the Internet."
- ONLINE BOOK INITIATIVE is an initiative formed to "make available freely redistributable collections of information." These collections include conference proceedings, various documents, and notably a number of full-text books, including authors such as Bierce, Dickens, Booker T. Washington, Pound, Chaucer, Thoreau, and others. Gopher to WORLD.STD.COM then choose "OBI The Online Book Initiative." Under "The Online Books" you will find a list of texts by author. (*Note:* Author names are alphabetical by first name.)

- OXFORD TEXT ARCHIVE consists of over 1,300 texts in 28 languages. The catalog and some of the texts are available by anonymous ftp to OTA.OX.AC.UK and at various gopher sites. For information you may send e-mail to the archive at ARCHIVE@VAX.OX.AC.UK.
- PROJECT GUTENBERG intends to make available a large number of public domain texts including numerous literary classics. It is available on many gophers. Further information can be obtained by subscribing to the Project Gutenberg newsletter, *GUTNBERG,* at LISTSERV@VMD.CSO.UIUC.EDU.
- RICE UNIVERSITY. "Information by Subject Area" at RICEINFO.RICE.EDU contains a menu selection for "Literature, Electronic Books and Journals" and is an exemplary location for numerous electronic texts. See Gopher Sites below.
- TEI. Text Encoding Initiative is a project to set SGML (Standard Generalized Markup Language) standards for electronic texts. TEI recently issued a new updated version of its guidelines. Guidelines are available in electronic form over the Internet. For more information contact the TEI editors by e-mail at TEI@UIC.EDU.
- UNIVERSITY OF MINNESOTA. The menu selection "Electronic books" is available under the "Libraries" menu at GOPHER.MICRO.UMN.EDU.
- THE WELL. This gopher for the Whole Earth 'Lectric Link (The Well) offers, as one might suspect, an unusual, eclectic, and distinctive selection of material. This includes electronic texts as well as information about printed texts. Two directories of special interest include "Authors, Books, Periodicals, Zines" and its subdirectory "Authors: Writings grouped by author name." GOPHER.WELL.SF.CA.US.
- WOMEN WRITERS PROJECT. The Women Writers Project at Brown University provides texts of some 200 literary works produced before 1830 by British, Scottish, Irish, and Welsh women writing in English, including works from other colonies. The WWP-L listserv offers a forum for discussion of the works. For further information about the archive contact the Women Writers Project at (401) 863-3619.

Fee-based services
ESTC. The Eighteenth-Century Short Title Catalogue is a project of the Research Libraries Group (RLG) and the International Committee of the Eighteenth-Century Short Title Catalogue (ESTC). When completed, ESTC will contain records for "virtually every English letterpress item published between 1473 and 1800." The catalog provides very detailed descriptions (not the texts themselves) for materials published in English and the other British languages anywhere in the world. For information contact the RLIN Information Center (BL.RIC@RLG.STANFORD.EDU) or the ESTC RLIN Liaison, Henry Snyder, at BM.ESL@RLG.STANFORD.EDU.

Gopher sites for general information
Many gopher sites have been suggested through the course of this resource list. The following is presented, however, for those who might wish a recommendation for a single gopher site to begin their explorations. RICEINFO. "Information by Subject Area" at RICEINFO.RICE.EDU contains a menu selections for "Literature, Electronic Books and Journals" which is an often-accessed and excellent starting point for anyone wishing to pursue gopher-accessible resources for English and American literature studies. Other menu selections of related interest under RiceInfo's "Information by Subject Area" are "Language and Linguistics" and "Film and Television."

Real-time conference facilities
Facilities are also available through the Internet for real-time conferencing in English and American literature studies through relevant MOOs. MOOs (multiple object-oriented) offer real-time discussions (that is, live and interactive, sometimes chatty) related to specific topics or themes.
- IATH-MOO: A Real-Time Multi-User Conference Facility. It includes linguistics, literary studies, medieval studies, teaching resources, and text-based virtual reality. Log in as a guest or mail a request for registration to IATH@VIRGINIA.EDU. To enter IATH-MOO telnet to HERO.VILLAGE. VIRGINIA.EDU 8888.
- PMC-MOO is a theoretical "environment" developed through the efforts of *Postmodern Culture*. It includes an interactive virtual library as well as a "theme park" and various areas for group discussion. Telnet to HERO.VILLAGE.VIRGINIA.EDU 7777.

The World Wide Web Virtual Library
General subject access
From the World Wide Web "Subject Catalogue" select "Literature and Art." Many subheadings relevant to English and American literature studies can be found under this heading. These include "English language Literature," "Project Gutenberg," "The Online Book Initiative," "The English Server" (which claims "many texts not available elsewhere on the Internet, primarily of interest to humanities scholars,") "Fiction," the "English Server" Poetry (a number of poems with keyword searching capability), "Contemporary Fiction" (a hypermedia exhibit), and *InterText Magazine*. The catalog's URL (case sensitive) is http://info.cern.ch/hypertext/DataSources/bySubject/Overview.html.

URLs of interest
- E-POETRY CENTER—RIF/T (BUFFALO). Electronic Poetics Center is a hypertextual gateway to "the extraordinary range of activity in formally

innovative writing in the United States and the world." Opening August 1, the center will provide access to numerous electronic resources in contemporary poetry including RIF/T. *Note:* A subscription to the E-Poetry list provides a subscription to E-Poetry Center announcements. Send E-Poetry subscriptions to LISTSERV@UBVM.CC.BUFFALO.EDU. The center's URL (case sensitive) is gopher://wings.buffalo.edu/11/internet/library/e-journals/ub/rift.

• INSTITUTE FOR ADVANCED TECHNOLOGY IN THE HUMANITIES. Recently added to the Web are the "First and Second Series of Research Reports" of the Institute. Its URL (case sensitive) is http://jefferson.village.virginia.edu.

• LABYRINTH. Global Information Network for Medieval Studies. Its URL (case sensitive) is http://www.georgetown.edu/labyrinth/labyrinth-home.html.

Reprinted from C&RL News, Vol. 55, No. 7, July/August 1994.

Internet resources for economics

Keith Morgan and Deborah Kelly-Milburn

Note: In all examples the home site of the information is given; however, many of these resources are "mirrored" at other sites or pointed to by local gophers. Check your local resources.

Economic indicators and reports

There are several excellent Internet collections of statistical data. This is an area that should significantly expand as more U.S. and, ideally, other national government information becomes Internet-accessible.

• Economic Bulletin Board (EBB): A first-rate example of an Internet resource that can be recommended as a research tool to patrons or used as a quick reference resource at an information desk. EBB offers the user access to thousands of data files, 700 of which are updated daily, in 22 different areas. The data are very diverse, covering such areas as employment statistics, energy shipments, the Survey of Current Manufactures datasheets, and U.S. dollar exchange rates at both 10 a.m. and 12 p.m. EST, Monday to Friday. A number of software programs to aid in both viewing and working with widescreen files are available from the ftp site in compressed, binary format.

EBB is available via the University of Michigan Libraries. Files are generally updated on a daily basis, whenever possible. Four file areas are emptied

Keith Morgan is reference librarian and economics subject specialist at the Massachusetts Institute of Technology, e-mail: kamorgan@mit.edu; Deborah Kelly-Milburn is research librarian, Research and Bibliography Services, Widener Library, Harvard University, e-mail: milburn@widener1.mbs.harvard.edu

at the beginning of each month; these are Trade Opportunity Program, USDA Agricultural Leads, International Market Insight Reports, and Eastern Europe Trade Leads. *Access:* Gopher "gopher.lib.umich.edu" /social sciences resources/ economics; *or:* Telnet "una.hh.lib.umich.edu" login as "gopher"; *or:* Anonymous ftp "una.hh.lib.umich.edu" /ebb/.

EBB is also available directly from the Department of Commerce for a fairly modest subscription fee. As of this writing this fee-based access method requires the user to search the Commerce bulletin board system, a method far less intuitive than gopher or ftp access, which will eventually be available directly from Commerce. *Access:* Telnet "ebb.stat-usa.gov" login as "guest".

• National Trade Data Bank (NTDB): This valuable collection of data has been available in CD-ROM format for several years; however, the Department of Commerce recently made it accessible via the Internet. Some of the many programs on NTDB include *The Foreign Trader's Index, Market Research Reports, The CIA World Factbook,* the complete text of the GATT and NAFTA agreements, and *U.S. Industrial Outlook.* There are plans for many other government agencies to disseminate information through NTDB. Among others, this includes the White House, the departments of State, Treasury, Defense, and Energy, the CIA, the International Trade Commission, and the Federal Reserve Board. There is a Web access point to NTDB, but this has been made a part of the subscription package. Gopher and ftp access remain free at the moment. *Access:* Gopher "gopher.stat-usa.gov"; *or:* WWW "http://www.stat-usa.gov/Ben/TradePromo.html"; *or:* Anonymous ftp "ftp.stat-usa.gov".

• EconData: This is an interesting supplement to EBB. EconData consists of several hundred thousand time series datasets from both U.S. national, state, local, and international sources. All data is in compressed zip format and mounted in the G data regression and model building program. There are three main file areas: Data, Tools, and Instructions. First-time users should get the files contents.doc, gbank.doc, and guide.doc from the Instructions directory. These files are all in ASCII format.

Examples of data available through EconData include the Annual Income and Product Accounts, Flow of Funds Accounts, Monthly National Employment, Hours, Earnings and Diffusion Indices, Producer Price and Consumer Price Indexes, and the blue pages from the *Survey of Current Business.* The essential advantages of EconData are the archival nature of its files and the standardized G Data-Bank format.

Unfortunately, accessing EconData via a Web browser requires putting in the very long URL listed below (note that there are no spaces at all in it). EconData has announced that the University of Maryland system presently requires this cumbersome process, but this will change soon. However, users can just put the URL into a browser once and then "bookmark" it in a Hotlist. *Access:* http://www.inform.edu/Educational_Resources/AcademicResourcesByTopic/EconomicsResources/EconData/econdata.html; *or:* Gopher "info.umd.edu"/EducationalResourcesEcon Data; *or:* Anonymous ftp to "info.umd.edu"/Info/EconData.

• NBER: The National Bureau of Economic Research gopher provides the Penn World Tables, an expanded dataset of international comparisons as well as an index of NBER publications. The ftp site also has the *Survey of Consumer Finances* (62–63; 83–86; 89), NBER trade and immigration data, the NBER Productivity Database, as well as other files. *Access:* Gopher "nber.harvard.edu"; *or:* Anonymous ftp "nber.harvard.edu"/pub/0.

• NEEEDC: The New England Electronic Economic Data Center offers the Federal Reserve Bank of New England's Economic Indicators (1969–). Also mounted at this site is the Regional Economic Information System (REIS) CD-ROM. The data are in .PRN format and can be read directly by Lotus or Quattro. *Access:* Anonymous ftp "neeedc.umesbs.maine.edu" "pass" for password cd frbb (for Reserve Bank Data) cd bea (for REIS).

• Dow-Jones: For a set of Dow-Jones historical averages three files are available: 1) Dow-Jones Industrial Averages, 1885–1985; 2) Date, high, low, and close for DJIA from 1952–1990; 3) DJIA close from 1900–1952. *Access:* Gopher "econ.lsa.umich.edu" /data/.

• Investment Data: This site contains some public domain investment finance data for the U.S. Although this is "unofficial" data, there are some interesting market data and programs. A partial listing of about 5,000 ticker symbols and a shareware copy of DC Econometrics' stock market forecasting models are just two examples of what is available here. *Access:* Anonymous ftp "dg-rtp.dg.com" /pub/misc.invest.

• SEC: The EDGAR project allows public access via the Internet to 10Q, 10K, and other financial disclosure information required by the SEC. The service is just getting started and not all companies are available; however, all publicly traded companies are required to file electronically by the end of 1995. This means that eventually this site will contain financial data for more than 15,000 companies. *Access:* Gopher "town.hall.org" /SEC Edgar; *or:* Anonymous ftp "townhall.org"/Edgar/; *or:* WWW "http://town.hall.org"/edgar/edgar.html/.

• Historic Price Data: A dataset of commodity price indexes from the U.K., U.S., Canada, Norway, and Sweden. U.K. numbers go back to 1600, the U.S. to 1790. All other countries complete from 1870 onwards. *Access:* Gopher "niord.shsu.edu" /economics/historic price data/.

• Statistics Canada Gopher: A new service as of February 1994, this site so far only lists the daily economic reports and the release data of new economic indicators. Available in English or French. *Access:* Gopher "talon. statcan.ca".

• Country Reports: The 4th annual *Economic Policy and Trade Practices* report from the U.S. Department of State provides detailed reports regarding the economic policies and trade practices of each country with which the U.S. has an economic or trade relationship. Each report is divided into nine areas and includes such information as key economic indicators, exchange rate policies, debt management policies, and an assessment of protections available for U.S. intellectual property. *Access:* Gopher "umslvma. umsl.edu" /library/govdocs/.

• Labor Statistics: LABSTAT, the Bureau of Labor Statistics' public database, provides current and historical data for 25 surveys. These include such databases as comprehensive *Consumer Price Index* data, *International Labor Statistics, The Producer Price Index,* and *Employment Cost Index.* See the file "overview.doc" in the "doc" directory for information on file storage. *Access:* Gopher: "hopi.bls.gov" *or:* Anonymous ftp "ftp.bls.gov" /pub/ time.series.

• Federal Reserve Bank: This site contains information from the Federal Reserve Board's statistical release series. Data such as the Flow of Funds Tables, Reserves of Depository Institutions, Selected Interest Rates, and other money stock measures and components are available. *Access:* Gopher "town.hall.org" /Federal Reserve; *or:* Anonymous ftp "townhall.org" /other/ fed/; *or:* WWW "http://town.hall.org/other/fed/".

• Social Security Administration: The electronic information system of the Office of Social Security offers the complete *Current Operating Statistics* from the *Social Security Bulletin* and selected information from the data tables in the *Annual Statistical Supplement. Access:* Gopher "oss968.ssa.gov"; *or:* Anonymous ftp "soaf1.ssa.gov"/pub/; *or:* WWW "http://www.ssa.gov/ SSA_Home.html".

• Federal Deposit Insurance Corporation: There are three valuable datasets on the FDIC gopher: *The Statistics on Banking, 1991; The Statistics on Banking, 1992; The Historical Statistics on Banking, 1934–1992.* Also, in the *Consumer Information Directory* is information on the Bank Rating Services, consumer rights, and insured deposits. Data files are primarily in Lotus 123 .WK1 format; text files are in both ASCII and WordPerfect 5.1. *Access:* Gopher "fdic.sura.net 71".

• The Bureau of the Census has an interesting collection of census data and other information available on its Webpage. Besides population data and research and methodology reports, particular files of interest are the

Statistical Abstract of the United States and a Collection of International Trade Statistics collected by the Bureau.
• Bank of England: The *Bank of England Quarterly Bulletin* time series data can be searched at this site. Access is very slow. *Access:* Telnet "sun.nsf.ac.uk" login: "janet" hostname: "uk.ac.swurcc" username: press [send] which service: PMAC [and] select 3 from the menu.
• U.K. Central Statistical Office: This site offers a search and extraction system for the Central Statistical Office's Macro-Economic Time Series data. Access is also very slow. *Access:* Telnet "sun.nsf.ac.uk" login "janet" hostname: "uk.ac.swurcc" username: press [send] which service: PMAC [and] select 1 from the menu.

Private datasets
An interesting use of the Internet has arisen as authors mount complementary economic datasets that relate to their own books and articles. Four recent examples are:
• John Abowd and Richard Freeman's edition of the NBER Project Research Report *Immigration, Trade and the Labor Market* (University of Chicago Press, 1991). *Access:* Gopher "nber.harvard.edu" /pub/trade.immigration.
• The dataset associated with David Backus and Patrick Kehoe's "International Evidence of the Historical Properties of Business Cycles," *American Economic Review* 82 (September 1992). *Access:* Anonymous ftp "uts.mcc.ac.uk" /pub/Krichel/DatEc.
• Gauss programs and datasets for count models and duration regression models associated with Gary Kig and Andrew Gelman's research, particularly in King's *Unifying Political Methodology* (Cambridge University Press, 1989). *Access:* Anonymous ftp "haavelmo.harvard.edu" pub/count; pub/judgeit; pub/maxlink.
• The Penn World Tables dataset discussed in Robert Summer and Alan Heston's "The Penn World Table (Mark 5): An Expanded Set of International Comparisons," *Quarterly Journal of Economics* 106 (May 1991). *Access:* Anonymous ftp "nber.harvard.edu /pub/pwt55/.

Software libraries
• Many economics articles are written with the LaTeX typesetting program. Several archive sites have style files that correspond with various journal requirements. Bibliographic style files for the *American Economic Review,* the *Canadian Journal of Economics,* and others are available. *Access:* Gopher "pip.shsu.edu" Economics/EconBib.
• The Netlib archive is a library of mathematical software and databases. The programs originated in various U.S. research labs and are generally of

very high quality. Most are written in Fortran but some other languages, particularly C and C++, are now available. Some well-known numerical software are on this site, including Linpack, Eispack, and Lapack. There are a number of sites available, several of which are listed below. *Access:* Gopher "wuecon.wustl.edu"/Washington University Economics Gopher/NetLib/; *or:* Anonymous ftp "netlib2.cs.utk.edu".

• The Statlib archive of statistical software contains a large collection of statistics, data, directory lists, and random material. Statlib contains the source code to entire statistics packages such as XlispStat. This site is probably not as valuable to economists as Netlib. *Access:* Gopher "lib.stat.cmu.edu"; *or:* ftp "lib.stat.cmu.edu" (login as "statlib", not anonymous).

Working papers
Like many academic disciplines, economics disseminates preliminary research through the preprint process of working papers. Several projects have begun to use the Internet as a wider and more efficient transmission medium. Three noteworthy projects are:

• The NetEc project: This is an attempt to assemble an extensive bibliography of current working papers in economics from departments all over the world (BibEc), in addition to an archive collection of the working papers (WoPEc). *Access:* Gopher "uts.mcc.ac.uk"/Economics—NetEc/; *or:* Telnet "uts.mcc.ac.uk" login in as "NetEc"; *or:* Anonymous ftp "uts.mcc.ac.uk"/pub/NetEc/.

• The Econ-wp archive: This is a project of the University of Washington at St. Louis that provides an Internet site for storing and accessing working papers in economics. The site is arranged according to the classification scheme from the *Journal of Economic Literature*. The Web server will display papers in PostScript format. *Access:* Gopher "econwpa.wustl.edu"; *or:* WWW "http://econwpa.wustl.edu/Welcome.html".

• The University of Michigan (UM) Department of Economics: This gopher server has a directory of UM department working papers as well as a directory of working papers related to the economics of the Internet. *Access:* Gopher "econ.lsa.umich.edu"/working papers/; *or:* WWW "http://gopher.econ.lsa.umich.eduEconInternet.html".

Newsgroups
The newsgroup "sci.econ" is the main Usenet Economics related newsgroup for general discussion. A moderated newsgroup, "sci.econ.research" was created in June 1993. Other newsgroups of interest to economists include:
• comp.text.tex: the TeX typesetting system
• misc.invest: investment finance

- sci.stat.math: statistics and math
- sci.stat.edu: statistics and education
- comp-soft.sys: SAS
- comp-soft.sys.spss: SPSS
- comp-soft.sys.shazam: the Shazam statistics package

• The archives of several groups can be found on the *Journal of Statistics Education* gopher at North Carolina State University. These include SAS-L; SPSSx-L; Stat-L; and Chance. *Access:* Gopher "jse.stat.ncsu.edu"/Other Discussion Groups/.

• For the archives of Pol-Econ and FedTax-L: *Access:* Gopher "niord.shsu. edu"/ Economics (SHSU Network Access Initiative Project)/Archives of Pol-Econ, FedTax-L, and sci.econ.research/.

Finding other resources

This is a very selective guide to resources on the Internet for economists. Since economics is such a pervasive discipline, you can be sure that the number of Internet resources will continue to grow. A guide such as this can only touch on some of the more pertinent sites; other guides are available on the network. A gopher at the University of Michigan maintains a clearinghouse of subject-oriented Internet resource guides, including several for economists. A particularly noteworthy guide is Bill Goffe's "Resources for Economists on the Internet." (*Access:* Gopher "una.hh.lib. umich.edu"/inetdirs.) For a Hypertext version of the same document: URL:http//gopher.lsa.umich.edu/EconFAQ/EconFAQ.html.

It is a sad fact of life on the network, however, that as soon as most guides are published, they are already out of date. For those who wish to search for current economics information on the Internet, gophers provide easy access. There are a number of gophers that have grouped information by subject (subject trees) and the gopher at Michigan State University provides an excellent starting place, connecting to over 20 different locations. The subject tree at Rice University is especially useful, with well over 100 resources accessible. (*Access:* Gopher "burrow.cl.msu.edu"/network & database resources/internet by subject.)

For the scholar searching for a particular piece of information on the Internet, Veronica and Jughead are the best tools for the novice. Both provide keyword indexing of gopher menus, allowing the user to pinpoint very specific information. Jughead searches only a specific group of gopher menus, and usually provides better, faster results. Veronica casts the widest possible net. Many gophers allow Veronica searches; the best site for Jughead is at Washington and Lee University. (*Access:* Gopher "liberty.uc.wlu.edu" / finding gopher resources/search high-level gopher menus by jughead.) The

Washington and Lee site is a very popular one and it is often difficult to connect directly to it. Sometimes accessing it through another site, such as U.C. Santa Cruz, works best. (*Access:* Gopher "scilibx.ucsc.edu" /the world/ other internet gopher servers/jughead.)

In order to make a comprehensive search of the Internet, the user must search Archie. Archie indexes the vast information residing at ftp sites around the globe. You can telnet to Archie sites at a variety of locations or submit requests by e-mail. In either case, Archie requires specific commands.

Reprinted from C&RL News, *Vol. 55, No. 8, September 1994. Revised January 1995.*

Internet resources for health and medicine

Lee Hancock

Internet use by health workers, and those interested in health issues, is growing rapidly. The number of new resources has expanded dramatically in the past year. Interfaces such as gopher and the World Wide Web (WWW) are making the Internet less cryptic, thus attracting large numbers of new users. Adding to this "structuring" is the use of subject trees to categorize resources. This article examines these medical resources as they are categorized by disease.

Non-disease-specific programs and documents
• HEALTHLINE. The University of Montana's Healthline service offers topics of general health interest. It covers topics of physical and mental health including sexuality, drug and alcohol information, academic tips, and dietary facts. *Access: URL:* gopher://selway.umt.edu:700/1.
• NLM's PRACTICE GUIDELINES-HSTAT. The National Library of Medicine (NLM) offers a free electronic resource which provides access to the full-text of clinical practice guidelines developed under the auspices of the Agency for Health Care Policy and Research (AHCPR). HSTAT also includes other documents useful in health care decision-making: National Institutes of Health (NIH) Consensus Statements, NIH Technology Assessments, and the U.S Preventive Services Task Force Guide to Clinical Preventive Services.

Lee Hancock is educational technologist at the University of Kansas Medical Center, Kansas City; Bitnet: LEO7144@KANVM; Internet: LEO7144@UKANVM.CC. UKANS.EDU

Access: Telnet: text.nlm.nih.gov *or URL:* http://www.nlm.nih.gov/, select NLM Online Information Services.

• MEDSEARCH AMERICA. This is the only national health care employment network on the Internet. Standard services to Healthcare Job Seekers are free of charge. *Access:* Gopher: Type=1, Name=MedSearch America, Path=, Host=gopher.medsearch.com, Port=9001 *or URL:* gopher://gopher.medsearch.com:9001/1; *e-mail:* office@medserch.com.

• THE VIRTUAL LIBRARY-MEDICINE. This is a comprehensive listing of WWW resources for biology and medicine. *Access:* World Wide Web, *URL:* http://golgi.harvard.edu/biopages/medicine.htm.

• THE VIRTUAL HOSPITAL. The Virtual Hospital (VH) is a continuously updated medical multimedia database stored on computers and accessed through high speed networks 24 hours a day. The VH will provide invaluable patient care support and distance learning to practicing physicians. *Access:* World Wide Web, *URL:* http://indy.radiology.uiowa.edu.Virtual Hospital.html; *e-mail:* librarian@indy.radiology.uiowa.edu.

Health resources categorized by disease
Menu trees are the current trend in trying to organize the perceived chaos of the Internet. Disease descriptions, treatment protocols, nursing information, news sources, and drug information are currently available. An excellent overall disease categorization on a gopher server is the Yale Biomedical Gopher of Diseases and Disorders. The server offers articles and resources on AIDS, cancer, diabetes, digestive disorders, and more. *Access: URL:* gopher://yaleinfo.yale.edu.

AIDS
• AIDS RELATED INFORMATION-NIAID GOPHER. This contains AIDSNews, CDC National AIDS Clearinghouse, and much more. *Access: URL:* gopher://odie.niaid.nih.gov/11.

• SOUTH EAST FLORIDA AIDS INFORMATION NETWORK. This database contains information on AIDS research organizations, and individuals working within these organizations located in southeastern Florida. Available information also includes educational and informational services on AIDS topics, health and social services, and research eligibility. This database was created with the help of the National Library of Medicine. *Access:* telnet 129.171.78.1, login: library, select L on main menu, select 1 on next menu.

• AIDS ALERT FOR HEALTH CARE WORKERS. This is an index to journal articles and occasional papers concerning the occupational health and safety issues of health care workers providing care to AIDS patients. The Alert is annotated and compiled by Charlotte Broome of the Ryerson Polytechnical

Institute's Education and Life Sciences Library. Issues of the Alert will appear three to four times per year. *Access:* The Alert is distributed electronically by the Institute for AIDS Information; *e-mail:* libr8508@ryerson. *Contact:* Bob Jackson, librarian for education and life sciences.

• AIDS. A listserv mailing list for the Sci.Med.AIDS Newsgroup. This is a redistribution list for the Usenet newsgroup Sci.Med.AIDS. Mail to the list is automatically forwarded to the moderator team for the newsgroup. *Subscribe:* LISTSERV@WUVMD.WUSTL.EDU *or* LISTSERV@WUVMD. *Contact:* Moderator team at aids@cs.ucla.edu.

• AIDSNEWS. The AIDSNews Forum is used for the discussion of any issue relating to AIDS/ARC. AIDS Treatment News reports on experimental and alternative treatments, especially those available now. *Subscribe:* LISTSERV@RUTGERS.EDU *or* LISTSERV@RUTVM1. *Contact:* Michael Smith; *e-mail:* msmith@umaecs.

Amyotrophic lateral sclerosis (ALS)

• ALS. This electronic mailing list has been set up to serve the worldwide ALS community. This includes ALS patients, ALS support/discussion groups, ALS clinics, ALS researchers, etc. Others are welcome to join. THIS IS NOT A LISTSERV SETUP. *Contact:* Bob Broedel; *e-mail:* bro@huey.met.fsu.edu.

• ALS DIGEST-Lou Gehrig's Disease. This electronic publication covers all aspects of Amyotrophic Lateral Sclerosis (ALS) or Lou Gehrig's Disease. This includes ALS patients, patient supporters, physicians, support groups, research centers, etc. To subscribe, unsubscribe, or to contribute notes, send e-mail to: Bob Broedel at bro@huey.met.fsu.edu.

Alzheimer's disease

• ALZHEIMER. ALZHEIMER is an e-mail discussion group for patients, professional and family caregivers, researchers, public policy makers, students, and anyone with an interest in Alzheimer's or related dementing disorders in older adults. ALZHEIMER is intended to provide interested individuals from various perspectives an opportunity to share questions, answers, suggestions, and tips. *Subscribe:* majordomo@wubios.wustl.edu and in the BODY of the message send the command: subscribe ALZHEIMER (no name necessary). *Contact:* ALZHEIMER-owner@wubios.wustl.edu.

Cancer

• BREAST CANCER INFORMATION CLEARINGHOUSE. The Breast Cancer Information Clearinghouse is an Internet-accessible resource for breast cancer patients and their families. Information currently available includes patient education materials from the American Cancer Society and the

National Cancer Institute, statistical information, and much more. *Access:* *Gopher:* nysernet.org *or URL:* http://nysernet.org. *Contact:*tmdamon@ nysernet.org.

• BREAST-CANCER. This is an open discussion list for any issue relating to breast cancer. It is an unmoderated list open to researchers, physicians, patients, family and friends of patients, for the discussion of related issues. *Subscribe:* LISTSERV@MORGAN.UCS.MUN.CA. *Contact:* Jon G. Church; e-mail: jchurch@kean.ucs.mun.ca.

• CANCERNET—GUIDE TO CANCER TREATMENT. This is a quick and easy way to obtain, through electronic mail, cancer information from the National Cancer Institute (NCI). CancerNet lets you request information statements from the NCI's Physician Data Query database, fact sheets on various cancer topics from the NCI's Office of Cancer Communications, and citations and abstracts on selected topics from the CANCERLIT database. Selected information is also available in Spanish. There is no charge for the service unless your local computer center charges for use of e-mail. The CancerNet contents list changes at the beginning of each month as new statements and other information is included. *Access:* 1) Address your mail message to: cancernet@icicb.nci.nih.gov. If you are not on Internet, you may have to change the format of the address. Consult your systems manager for the correct address format. 2) In the body of the message: a) if you need the CancerNet contents list, enter "help" to receive the most current list (substitute the word "spanish" for "help" if you want the contents list in Spanish). For example: cancernet@icicb.nci.nih.gov, subject: help <This is the body of the message>; b) if you have the CancerNet contents list and would like to request a particular statement or piece of information, enter the code from the contents list for the desired information. If you want more than one piece of information, enter the code for each piece of information desired on a separate line within the message. *Note:* Individual statements may exceed 100K and some mail systems are limited in the size of the mail messages a user can receive. Please check your mail and storage capacity prior to submitting requests.

The information in CancerNet is also available on several gopher servers as well as a number of secondary distributor sites. To access a gopher server if you have gopher client software on your host computer or PC, point to gopher.nih.gov. CancerNet can also be accessed via telnet: gopher.ncc.go.jp (160.190.10.1), using "gopher" as the logon and password (additional gopher public access sites can also be accessed via telnet). You may have to go through several menus and submenus to access CancerNet on a gopher server. For a complete listing of all gopher and secondary sites, request item cn-400030 from CancerNet.

If you have any further questions, call: (301) 496-7403 or send an Internet message to Cheryl Burg, CancerNet project manager, at: cheryl@icicb.nci.nih. gov.

- ONCOLINK—U. OF PENN MULTIMEDIA ONCOLOGY RESOURCE. OncoLink is a WWW server and gopher server oriented to cancer. This resource is directed to physicians, health care personnel, social workers, patients and their supporters. *Access:* World Wide Web, *URL:* http:// cancer.med.upenn.edu. *Contact:* E. Loren Buhle Jr.; *e-mail:* buhle@xrt.upenn. edu.
- CER-L. This electronic discussion list is a public group for the discussion of cancer-related topics. *Subscribe:* LISTSERV@WVNVM.WVNET.EDU *or* LISTSERV@WVNVM. *Contact:* Susan Rodman; e-mail: u0ac3@wvnvm.bitnet.

Diabetes
- DIABETES. This is an International Research Project on Diabetes discussion group. *Subscribe:* LISTSERV%IRLEARN.bitnet@HEARN.nic.SURFnet.nl *or* LISTSERV@IRLEARN. *Contact:* Martin Wehlou; *e-mail:* wehlou@fgen. rug.ac.be.
- DIABETIC. This forum is open to all users on this and any other node to aid diabetic persons in the exchange of views, problems, anxieties, and other aspects of their condition. As this is a public forum, all messages are subject to review by anyone who might request a copy. *Subscribe:* LISTSERV%PCCVM.BITNET@cmsa.BerKeywordsley.EDU *or* LISTSERV@ PCCVM. *Contact:* R. N. Hathhorn; *e-mail:* sysmaint@pccvm.

Lyme disease
- LYMENET-L. Subscribers to LymeNet-L receive the *LymeNet Newsletter* about twice a month. This publication provides readers with the latest research, treatment and political news about the lyme disease epidemic. *Contact:* Marc Gabriel, editor-in-chief, the *LymeNet Newsletter;* e-mail: mcg2@lehigh.edu.

Multiple sclerosis
- MSLIST-L. The multiple sclerosis discussion list. *Subscribe:* LISTSERV%TECHNION.AC.IL@VM.TAU.AC.IL *or* LISTSERV@TECHNION.

Conclusion
There are also entry points to specialty-based medical knowledge on Internet. Computer departments, medical schools, and infomatics programs tend to develop information sources. Medical specialties are just beginning to take an interest in the Internet. An example is the Global Emergency Medicine

Archives which includes an online emergency medical journal. *Access:* World Wide Web, *URL:* http://herbst7.his.ucsf.edu.

Thomas Jefferson University (TJU) and the previously mentioned Yale offer access to medical information by specialty and topic. These are good starting points for exploration of medical Internet resources and give a good sense of their scope. TJU offers gopher topic categorized medical knowledge. The gopher allows a hypertext access to worldwide servers related to topics such as AIDS, biology, cancer, diabetes, disability information, epidemiology, etc. *Access:* World Wide Web, *URL:* gopher://tjgopher.tju.edu/11/medical/bytopic *or gopher:* tjgopher.tju.edu.

Of course, it's beyond the scope of this article to list all health resources available on the Internet. There are over 300 listserv lists alone. Over the years this author has cataloged about 700k worth of resources in a document titled *Internet/Bitnet Health Science Resources*. It covers a vast array of listservs lists, newsgroups, e-publications, databases, gophers, WWW servers, and much more. The document is available via anonymous ftp from ftp2.cc.ukans.edu in the directory pub/hmatrix as the file medlstxx.txt *or* .zip. The xx in the address is the date of the release and will change with updates.

Reprinted from C&RL News, *Vol. 55, No. 9, October 1994. Revised January 1995.*

First Peoples and the Internet

Gladys Smiley Bell

Electronic access to research and interactive communication for and about Native Americans is available in a variety of ways, and growing dramatically in number and scope. What was once an esoteric tool used only by scientists and engineers, the Internet is now having a dramatic impact on ethnic cultures, including Native Americans. Throughout this overview of Native American resources on the Internet the terms Native North Americans, Indians, American Indians, Native Americans, Aboriginal peoples, first peoples, and others are used interchangeably.

The information superhighway trek begins by accessing a document entitled "Public Access to the Internet: American Indian and Alaskan Native Issues" by George D. Baldwin (Henderson State University). Baldwin helped launch American Telecommunications (AIT), the first nonprofit group dedicated to promoting the grassroots Native American computing movement.[1] The document provides a historical and critical overview of communication, technology, and Indian Culture. *Access: URL:* ftp://ftp.NIC.MERIT.EDU/conference.proceedings/harvard.pubaccess.symposium/network.communities/networking.nations.txt.

Electronic discussion lists

• AISESnet. American Indian Science and Engineering Society (AISES) Network. This electronic list provides communication and information for AISES

Gladys Smiley Bell is coordinator of electronic information services at Kent State University Libraries, Ohio; e-mail: gbell@kentvm.kent.edu

chapters, students and faculty associated with AISES, and for members of industry and government. AISES membership is open to all, including non-AISES members. The list is divided into four groups: 1) AISESnet general: topics include AISES issues, position openings, scholarship announcements, AISES chapter communications, conference information, AISES events and announcements, powwow information, topics of general interest, and chapter newsletters; 2) AISESnet Discussion: intended for the discussion of Native American issues, engineering and science issues, public opinion, creative writing, etc.; 3) Alcohol & Drug: deals only with drug- and alcohol-related issues, and will provide information as well as support; participation is anonymous and return address labels will not be shown in the messages sent out by AISESnet; 4) AISESnet Drums: a distribution list dedicated to drum groups, it will only deal with issues concerning drum groups, powwow drum groups, drum building, powwow singers, etc.

When you subscribe to AISESnet, you will be added automatically to the AISESnet General and AISESnet Discussions lists. You must indicate that you would like to subscribe to the AISESnet Drums and/or the Alcohol & Drug list as well. There are four AISESnet gopher databases: student resumes, AISESnet membership directory, job listings, and submissions (archives). *Access:* aisesnet@selway.umt.edu. *Based on information provided by Borries Demeler, AISESnet listowner; demeler@ selway.umt.edu.*

• INDIANnet. Census Information and Computer Network Center. This is the first national computer listserv to provide civic information useful to American Indian and Alaskan Natives. Services include computer conferences and private electronic mail for Indian tribes, nonprofit organizations, and individuals. It includes federal information such as the *Federal Register,* Employment Opportunities, Environmental Protection Agency data, U.S. Census data and Geographic Information System (TIGER) files. There is also a specialized collection of American Indian and Alaskan Native research reports extracted from the Educational Research Information Clearinghouse (ERIC). There is an amazing collection of authentic electronic Indian artwork and graphics. The most ambitious project is the Tribal Profiles Database. *Access:* listserv@spruce.hsu.edu. *Based on information provided by George Baldwin, INDIANnet director; baldwin@holly.hsu.edu.*

• INDKNOW. For discussion of Indigenous Knowledge Systems. *Access:* listserv@uwavm.u.washington.edu.

• IROQUOIS. Iroquoian Language discussion. *Access:* listserv@vm.utcc. utoronto.edu.

• NativeNet. An overlapping set of electronic discussion lists that also have overlapping memberships and are organized by topic. NAT-1492 is a

Columbus quincentenary mailing list dealing specifically with the 500th anniversary of Columbus's voyage to the "New World," and the havoc that ensued for the native people of the Americas. *Access:* listserv@tamvm1.tamu.edu. NATCHAT provides a forum for general discussion pertaining to indigenous people of the world. *Access:* listserv@tamvm1.tamu.edu. NATIVE-L, Indigenous Peoples Information, provides a general forum for exchanging information and perspectives on matters relating to the indigenous people of the world. *Access:* listserv@tamvm1.tamu.edu. (NATIVE-L and NATCHAT are "gatewayed" with the soc.culture.native Usenet newsgroup in such a way that any message posted to soc.culture.native will be sent to a NativeNet moderator who (if s/he approves) will relay the posting to either the NATIVE-L or NATCHAT mailing list. Any message posted to mailing addresses attached to these two lists will automatically be sent to soc.culture.native.) NAT-HLTH, Health Issues of Native Peoples. *Access:* listserv@tamvm1.tamu.edu. NAT-LANG, a discussion list for exchanging information concerning the languages of indigenous people. *Access:* listserv@tamvm1.tamu.edu. NAT-EDU deals with issues regarding the provision of culturally sensitive educational programs for native people and better and more accurate educational materials concerning native people for mainstream students. *Access:* listserv@indycms.iupui.edu. *Based on information provided by Gary Trujillo, NativeNet listowner; gst@gnosy.svle.ma.us.*

• NATIVE-LIT-L. Native American Literature by autochthonous people of the North Americas (the U.S., Canada, and Mexico) and neighboring islands, including Hawaii. Discussions are open to any aspect of native literature as well as book reviews; articles about poetry, fiction, and criticism; information about publications, talks, and conferences; and general chitchat about native literature. *Access:* listserv@cornell.edu. *Based on information provided by Michael Wilson, Native-Lit-L listowner; idoy@crux1.cit.cornell.edu.*

• NativeProfs-L. Private electronic list for the Association of American Indian & Alaskan Native Professors.

• NIPC. National Indian Policy Research Institute Electronic Clearinghouse. An information clearinghouse on a wide range of policy issues to the 500 U.S. Native American tribes since 1990. *Access:* listserv@gwuvm.gwu.edu.

Anonymous ftp site
• alt.native-ftp-site. Contains documents pertaining to Native Americans. *Access: URL:* ftp://ftp.cit.cornell.edu/pub/special/NativProfs/usenet.

Gopher sites
• Native American Net Server. Server home for files pertaining to Native Americans. The bulletin board system is also available for posting notices about things for sale and upcoming events. *Access: URL:* gopher://alpha1.csd.uwm.edu/UW M Information/The Native American Net.
• UC-Berkeley Library gopher. Native American Studies Section. *Access: URL:* gopher://infolib.lib.berkeley.edu, port 70/Research Databases and Resources by Subject/Ethnic Studies/Native American Studies.

UseNet newsgroups
Local computer services staff should be consulted to find out what the availability and procedures are for access to: alt.native, soc.culture.indian.american, soc.culture.native.american.

World Wide Web Sites
• Native American Resources on the Internet *Access:* http: //hanksville.phast.umass.edu/misc/NAresources.html
• The NativeNet Information Network *Access:* http: //kuhttp.cc.ukans.edu/~marc/

Other significant electronic resources
• ACTIV-L. Activists for peace, empowerment, human rights, justice, etc. *Access:* listserv@mizzou1.missouri.edu.
• Educational Native American Network (ENAN). Call (505) 277-7310 for password and 800 number for dial-in access and information. (Scheduled soon for Internet access.) Established by and for the Bureau of Indian Affairs (BIA) and the Office of Indian Education Programs (OIEP) schools serving American Indian children. The network provides teachers with access to a wide range of information on technical assistance and training resources. Through the network, teachers are able to share information on effective practices and classroom ideas; access curriculum materials and resources related to Indian education from universities, museums, etc.; and take online courses. It also supports multiple classroom site instructional projects.
• Molis. Minority Online Information Service. Provides comprehensive information on Native American, black, and Hispanic minority colleges and universities. *Access: URL:* ftp://ftp.fie.com or *URL:* gopher://gopher.fie.com or *URL:* telnet://fedix.fie.com or *URL:* http://www.fie.com.
• ORTRAD-L. Discussion regarding studies in oral tradition for all those interested in the world's living oral traditions (e.g., African, Hispanic, Native American, etc.). *Access:* listserv@mizzou1.missouri.edu.

Conclusion

Taking a hike using Veronica to search gopher sites revealed all of the above information. For more information on electronic resources for Native Americans take a ride on the information superhighway using gopher, Mosaic, Cello, or Lynx, and consult the following:

• Directory of Scholarly Electronic Conferences. 8th Revision. listserv@kentvm.kent.edu (get acadlist file<no.>) or *URL:* ftp:ksuvxa.kent.edu/library.

• Art McGee. NatvInfo. *Access: URL:* ftp://ftp.netcom.com/pub/amcgee/indigenous/my_indigenous_related_lists.

Note

1. A. J. S. Rayl, "New technologies, ancient cultures; use of computer and information technology by Native Americans," *Omni* 15 (August 1993): 46–48.

Reprinted from C&RL News, *Vol. 55, No. 10, November, 1994. Revised January 1995.*

Internet resources for the space sciences

Robert Pasicznyuk

In the coming decade, NASA expects to download a terabyte of information each day from its space station roughly equivalent to 71 billion floppy disks or 15 billion compact discs. The deluge of tomorrow has a harbinger today in the wealth of information opportunities in the space sciences on the Internet. Internet aerospace and astrophysics sources offer a mix of traditional text databases, high resolution graphics archives, news services, and discussion lists. Like other information in electronic formats, space sciences sources on the Net have the advantage of being continually updated and augmented. The varied formats present media ready for personal manipulation, analysis, and enjoyment..

Space sciences sources on the Internet offer an array of text, auditory, and graphic information. File types/formats are legion and growing. To take full advantage of multimedia sites requires both the computer hardware and software appropriate to the formats. A fully capable multimedia system will include a variety of viewers (graphics, sound, and video), a sound card or speaker drivers, and a high resolution monitor. If your system lacks some or all of these capabilities, take advantage of those that your system can handle. There are still many text-based systems on the net. You may also want to use computing's advance in multimedia as justification to upgrade your system. Increasingly popular Internet programs, such as *Mosaic* and *Netscape*, are ideal for getting the most out of multimedia net

Robert W. Pasicznyuk is sciences subject specialist at the University of Colorado at Colorado Springs; e-mail: rwpasicznyuk@uccs.edu

opportunities. One of the givens of multimedia computing is that the files are large. Collectors interested in gathering files must have sufficient storage to handle the load.

Resources Accessible Via Telnet and FTP

• CASS: Center for Advanced Space Studies. Cass offers text and graphic information from numerous NASA projects. Contributors include the Lunar and Planetary Institute (LPI), the Exploration Science Institute (ESI), NASA's Division of Educational Programs (DEP), and NASA libraries. Through CASS, users can find announcements of astrophysics and astronomy professional meetings, read articles from the *Lunar and Planetary Bulletin,* or consult several indexes and reference works. CASS also acts as a gateway to the Lunar & Planetary Bibliography, library catalogs, and the Image Retrieval and Processing System. *Access via telnet:* cass.jsc.nasa.gov; Login as cass (lowercase); the password is online. *Note:* The "About CASS" option is invaluable for navigating the system.

• NASA SPACELINK. Spacelink provides a wealth of text reports covering NASA projects both past and present. In addition to astronomy and astrophysics information, users can display files covering the environment, the history of space exploration, space shuttle flight information, NASA plans for the future, and fact sheets. Spacelink also provides image files (GIF format). Look for images of the comet Shoemaker-Levy 9's impact with Jupiter. *Access via telnet:* spacelink.msfc.nasa.gov; login as guest. *Access via FTP:* spacelink.msfc.nasa.gov; anonymous login

• NED: NASA Extragalactic Database. NED allows users to search celestial objects, data, and literature. Information about objects is accessible by object name, position, and skyplot. Search parameters also include catalog and photometry. NED acts as a current awareness service providing contents and abstracts information from prominent astronomy and astrophysics journals. Searching the journal contents, abstracts, and dissertations/thesis options will become apparent to anyone who has searched similar databases. The other options require facility with astronomy nomenclature and designations. More information about NED is available in Egret and Albrecht's *Databases and Online Data in Astronomy.* Page 91 contains a discussion of *NED. Access via telnet:* ned.ipac.caltech.edu; login as ned

• NODIS: National Space Science Data Center. NODIS is a gateway for space science data in the topics of astrophysics, space physics, planetary sciences, earth sciences, microgravity, and spacecraft. NODIS also provides a catalog of NASA CD-ROMs with ordering capability. Users

can view sample images of the CDs if they have graphics capability. Graphics can also be downloaded and retrieved by anonymous FTP. NODIS files are in GIF, Postscript, RTF, and ASCII formats. *Access via telnet:* nssdca.gsfc.nasa.gov; login as nodis. *Access via FTP:* nssdc.gsfc.nasa.gov; anonymous login
- Space Shuttle Earth Observations Project. Sponsored by the Johnson Space Center, Houston, Texas, The Space Shuttle Earth Observations Project provides access to image files of selected photographs taken by Space Shuttle astronaut crews. The files are available for downloading via FTP, KERMIT, or E-Mail (MIME encoded). Searchers can view a list of all images or search them by mission, geographical coordinates, or combination. *Access via telnet:* sseop.jsc.nasa.gov; username photos. *Access via FTP:* sseop.jsc.nasa.gov; anonymous login

Resources Accessible Via the World Wide Web
- ADS: NASA Astrophysics Data System Server. The NASA Astrophysics Data System Server aims at making NASA space missions information available to astronomers. ADS supplies software allowing users to make complex operations and manipulations on NASA data sets.
Sample questions that can be answered through ADS include:
What supernova remnant images are available in the X-ray wavelength band?
What sites have catalogs of observational data? Are the observations available?
ADS also provides access to its home page, tutorial, and registration. The home page supplies information about the system and acts as a gateway to other Internet space sciences sources. ADS allows searching of 160,000 abstracts produced in the NASA/STI project, access to an archive of data collected by the Einstein X-ray satellite mission, and access to about 150 astronomical catalogs. The home page describes how to register for ADS software. *Access:* http://adswww.colorado.edu
- CASS: Center for Advanced Space Studies. The CASS http server offers a detailed description of the research opportunities afforded by CASS (see telnet resources for description), a telnet link to the CASS, a copy of the *Lunar and Planetary Information Bulletin,* and a link to the CASS gopher. *Access:* http://cass.jsc.nasa.gov/CASS_home.html
- NASA SPACELINK. With the addition of a point-and-click interface, the Spacelink http server provides the same kinds of information as its text-based counterpart (see telnet resources for a complete description). This is just the kind of Internet source that makes Mosaic, Netscape, and analogues shine. *Access:* http://spacelink.msfc.nasa.gov.

- The NASA General Information Server. The mother of all NASA http servers, the NASA General Information Server provides a wealth of NASA news, information, and links to specific sites. Here is a sample of the choices you will encounter:

Hot Topics—NASA news and subjects of public interest
NASA's Strategic Plan, Specific NASA Strategies & Policies
NASA Public Affairs
NASA Online Educational Resources
NASA Centers (Accessible by Geographic Location)
Guide to NASA Online Resources
    NASA Online Information
    NASA Personnel Lookup
    NASA-Wide Programs
    NASA Technical Report Server
    NASA Commercial Technology

Access: http://hypatia.gsfc.nasa.gov/NASA_homepage.html

- NASA Web Servers by Center. Many, if not all of the NASA centers have their own home pages. The centers often describe their mission, history, and research goals. They also provide lookup facilities for personnel, facilities maps, and center publications. Some supply links to data sets, libraries, images, and other sites.
- NASA Ames Research Center. *Access:* http://www.arc.nasa.gov/
- NASA Dryden Flight Research Center. *Access:* http://www.dfrf.nasa.gov/dryden.html
- NASA Goddard Institute for Space Studies. *Access:* http://www.giss.nasa.gov/
- NASA Goddard Space Flight Center. *Access:* http://www.gsfc.nasa.gov/GSFC_homepage.html
- NASA Jet Propulsion Laboratory. *Access:* http://www.jpl.nasa.gov/
- NASA Johnson Space Center. *Access:* http://www.jsc.nasa.gov/jsc/home.html
- NASA Kennedy Space Center. *Access:* http://www.ksc.nasa.gov/ksc.html
- NASA Langley Research Center. *Access:* http://www.larc.nasa.gov/larc.html
- NASA Lewis Research Center. *Access:* http://www.lerc.nasa.gov/LeRC_homepage.html
- NASA Marshall Space Flight Center. *Access:* http://www.msfc.nasa.gov/
- NASA Stennis Space Center. *Access:* http://moses.ssc.nasa.gov/
- NASA Wallops Flight Facility. *Access:* http://hypatia.gsfc.nasa.gov/WFF_infopage.html
- NASA Scientific and Technical Information Program. The Scientific and Technical Information Program Server provides access to NASA databases,

Selected Current Aerospace Notices (SCAN), the NASA Thesaurus, and a WAIS searchable file of NASA RECON. The server also includes links to additional databases (RECON and ARIN) and access to several Internet search engines. *Access:* http://www.sti.nasa.gov/STI-homepage.html

• STEIS: Space Telescope Electronic Information Service. This STEIS http Server is one-stop-shopping for information from and about the Hubble Space Telescope. It provides general and background information about STEIS and astrophysics scholarship: organization news, libraries, the STEIS phone book, a record of STEIS staff research, access to publications of the Astronomical Society of the Pacific (PASP), a guide to star catalogs and sky surveys, a job posting, listing of meetings, workshops, talks, and colloquia, and STEIS visitor information. The server also supplies searchers with Hubble pictures, animations, and instructional materials. The STEIS server describes submission information for researchers who wish to use Hubble and includes an archive of space telescope data. *Access:* http://marvel.stsci.edu

Resources Accessible via Gopher

• NASA Center for Aerospace Information Gopher. The CASS gopher counterpart to information accessible via WWW and telnet. The gopher includes access to *Selected Current Aerospace Notices* (SCAN), NASA's library network (ARIN), STI program groups, a searchable 1990-1994 subset of the RECON database, and other aerospace Internet resources. *Gopher to:* gopher://gopher.sti.nasa.gov:70/1

• NASA, High Energy Astrophysics Science Archive Research Center, On-Line Data and Software. *Gopher to:* gopher://heasarc.gsfc.nasa.gov:70/1

• NASA SPACELINK. Gopher access to NASA news, information, and educational services. (See telnet resources for a complete description of SPACELINK) *Gopher to:* spacelink.msfc.nasa.gov

• STEIS: Space Telescope Electronic Information Service. The Space Telescope Information System gopher supplies the same kind of information as its http counterpart (See World Wide Web Resources for a detailed description). *Gopher to:* stsci.edu

Resources for News and Discussion

• Hubble Telescope Bulletin Board Daily and Status Reports. This BBS lists Hubble status reports, scheduled activities, and tasks accomplished. *Access:* Telnet to *STINFO.HQ.ESO.ORG*; login as *stinfo* (lower case)

• SpaceNews. Not a listserv or BBS, SpaceNews is a news and information service available weekly via the Amateur Packet Radio Network (AMPR), AMSAT-OSCAR-16, and the Usenet newsgroups of rec.radio.amateur.space, rec.radio.amateur.misc, rec.radio.amateur.info, and sci.space.news. Archives are available via anonymous FTP at pilot.njin.net in the pub/SpaceNews subdirectory. It originates at KD2BD in Wall Township, New Jersey, USA and is made available for unlimited free distribution. *Access:* Finger magliaco@pilot.mjin.net for current news. *Contact:* kd2bd@ka2qhd.de.com -or-kd2bd@amsat.org for more information.

• NASA Headline News. This news service is provided by the Microwave Subnode of NASA's Planetary Data System. It provides NASA news bulletins, current information, and mission status reports. *Access:* finger nasanews@space.mit.edu; E-Mail listserver at pds-listserver@space.mit.edu; anonymous ftp is available at delcano.mit.edu; and a WWW home page at http://delcano.mit.edu. NASA press releases and other information are available automatically by sending an Internet electronic mail message to domo@hq.nasa.gov. In the body of the message (not the subject line) users should type the words subscribe press-release.

• SPACEMET: Science and Space Bulletin Board. SpaceMet is sponsored by the Department of Physics and Astronomy of the University of Massachusetts, Amherst, the National Science Foundation, and MassNet. It provides a forum for discussing space sciences issues. Although this BBS is geared toward K-12 students and teachers, many of the discussions are appropriate for students and faculty at the collegiate level who have interest in the subject. *Access:* Telnet to SPACEMET.PHAST.UMASS.EDU.

• SCI.ASTRO.HUBBLE Newsgroup. The forum originally intended to center on the processing of data taken with the Hubble Space Telescope (HST). It has become an instrument for the dissemination of information about the operations and status of HST. The newsgroup also serves as a platform for problems, requests, suggestions, and needs of the scientific community as they use the telescope for research purposes. *Contact:* scowen@wfpc3.la.asu.edu for information and article submission.

Reprinted from C&RL News, Vol. 55, No. 11, December 1994. Revised January 1995.